Information

Information

KING SOLOMON SPIRITUAL LIBRARY
THE GOD ENCYCLOPAEDIA WORD OF INFINITY

BY
THE SPIRIT OF THE FATHER GOD
THROUGH HIS SERVANT
HRM KING SOLOMON DAVID JESSE ETE
(King Solomon Spiritual Library)
Eteroyal Universal Family - BCS

All rights reserved
Copyright © Solomon ETE, 2008
Solomon ETE is hereby identified as author of this work in accordance with Section 77 of the Copyright, Designs and Patents Act 1988

The book cover picture is copyright to Solomon ETE

This book is published by
King Solomon Spiritual Library
P O BOX 27394
London E12 6WW UK
www.kingsolomonspirituallibrary.com

This book is sold subject to the conditions that it shall not, by way of trade or otherwise, be lent, resold, hired out or otherwise circulated without the author's or publisher's prior consent in any form of binding or cover other than that in which it is published and without a similar condition including this condition being imposed on the subsequent purchaser.

A CIP record for this book is available from the British Library
ISBN 978-0-9559801-8-3

INFORMATION
REPORT AND REPORTERS

= = = = =

"THE SUPREME ECHO OF LIFE"

Information

Contents

Part One: ***11-34***

INTRODUCTION

A: What is information?

B: What is report?

C: Who are reporters?

D: The word of everlasting record

E: This is good news to all mankind

F: Blessed are those who will use this information and change the world

G: I am the supreme introducer of life

Part Two: **35-58**
INFORMATION

A: what is information?

B: The supreme intelligent spirit gen

C: The genesis of all things

D: The bubble of creation

E: The servant of the word is information

F: Why the word lives in every person

G: Human is a distribution centre for all type of information

Part Three   **59-89**
REPORT

a: what is report

B: Information also means report

C: An official report

D: Non-official report

E: Evil people like report

F: The sign of a good leader

G: Do not need a report from humans if you are a good leader

Part Four 90-113
REPORTERS

A: What is a reporter?

B: Who reports whom?

C: The work of Satan is to report

D: The positive and negative newscaster

E: Evil people live by information from man's report

F: Spiritual reporters

G: What kind of a reporter are you

Part Five   **114-127**
CONCLUSION

A: The supreme reporter is the holy sprit of truth

B: Evil reporters are the workers of Satan

C: **I AM THE FATHER GOD**, **I** judge according to what **I** hear and know and see.

Chapter Two   **128-198**
MY OFFICE

Chapter Three   **199-236**
INSPIRATIONAL WRITER

Information

INFORMATION

PART ONE:
INTRODUCTION

FATHER'S TALK
(GOD PRESENT)

**Moses, Nineteenth, John FATHER, Two Thousand and Seven (AI/OG/BOOG)
Thursday, Nineteenth July,
Year Two Thousand
and Seven (19/07/2007)**

In the Name of Our Lord Jesus Christ, In the Blood of Our Lord Jesus Christ Now and forever more

Today, it pleases **ME, THE FATHER GOD THE CREATOR OF THE UNIVERSE** to give this Lecture

Revelation. The title is **INFORMATION, REPORT AND REPORTERS.** This Lecture Revelation will consist of Part One, Part Two, Part Three, Part Four and Part Five.

A: **WHAT IS INFORMATION?**

INFORMATION is THE SPIRIT itself. **I, THE FATHER GOD** from the beginning of time is **INFORMATION**. The Supreme Energy that is generating in **ME** called The Genesis of All Things - Motive and Effort, the Motivated Energy of **THE FATHER GOD**, the Light **HIMSELF** is **INFORMATION**, when we talk about the Spoken Word - the **WORD** that is **INFORMATION.**

In spirit the first power of the **WORD** is the energy called *'GEN'* **INFORMATION,** which is the Centre of Operations. That is exactly what **INFORMATION** stands for. As you can see, the control key of every rulership, every management, company, States, Countries, Nation, which is the light of everywhere via **The Word** is **INFORMATION**. This **INFORMATION** must be positive because that is where the energy of **THE FATHER GOD** is based. Without the **INFORMATION *ENERGY*** the world would still be in silence.

INFORMATION is the centre of advertisement. It is the meaning of pronouncements, the Spoken. That is the energy of **INFORMATION. *Ting*** and ***vowel*** are the vocabularies that give meaning to every word. The informant, **informing**, tell me. That is the meaning of **INFORMATION**. It is plural.

INFORMATION of God is the Holy Spirit, the Word of God. What we called the Word of God is **INFORMATION.** The Holy Bible contains the Word of Holy Writ from prophets of God, which were inspired by the positive words. That is the Centre of **INFORMATION.**

Information

From this Generation and of Everlasting age of Glorious testimony of **THE FATHER GOD** means The **WORD**. The **INFORMATION CENTRE** OF **THE WORD** IS KING SOLOMON SPIRITUAL LIBRARY.

I AM THE INFORMATION SELF. THE **WORD IS MYSELF,** but the above is where **I** kept the information – **THE COMPREHENSIVE AND ABILITY MEMORY OF THE FATHER GOD,** but the power of bringing things out from **MY** innersole self to the hearing of humanity is the energy of **THE FATHER GOD'S INFORMATION BANK** itself.

THE FATHER GOD INFORMATION CENTRE must be established in every situation and all aspect of lives. If **I** don't give this Lecture Revelation it means **I** have not (posterized) earmark or reveal the actual meaning of King Solomon Spiritual Library. It means **INFORMATION CENTRE OF THE FATHER GOD.** There are so many sub – sub **INFORMATION CENTRE OF GOD.** Every human being that can speak positive **WORD**, especially the ordain prophet of God are all **INFORMATION CENTRE.**

What the mind – the Supreme Mind, the thought or any spirit soul wants to bring out to the hearer must come from man and it is via the Word. When the WORD wanted to manifest HIS glory through **THE FATHER GOD'S** INNERSOLES, which is the **THOUGHT**, the **SON** is THE SUPREME WORD and **INFORMATION** is the Servant. So in an indirect way this Lecture stands for King Solomon ETE THE SERVANT OF THE WORD. He is the **INFORMATION CENTRE** where you can get this **FATHER'S TALK (GOD PRESENT).**

INFORMATION is another SUPER ENERGY, an entity that **I** created as a Spiritual soul of human-God and whoever that stands for **INFORMATION** is a servant of THE SUPREME WORD – a servant of God.

All prophets are servants of God. All the negative human beings are evil agents as information centre for evil.

I AM giving this information today so that you are careful whom you represent. Every person that speaks is an information centre. You are either positive or negative information centre. That is Introduction Part A of this Lecture Revelation.

B: **WHAT IS REPORT?**

Report is the urge, the ability to give out information. If you hear something, you keep it to yourself. But if you do not want to keep it to yourself, you give out the information. That is the energy of Report.

It is either the Report is needed or it is not needed. The report itself is the **INFORMATION** and that is the WORD **HIMSELF.** That is the reason **I** said everything is one. Everything is interwoven in oneness. The SPIRIT, which is **THE FATHER GOD,** is about the **WORD**, which is **THE FATHER**

GOD'S SOLE ENERGY. It is also about **INFORMATION,** which is **THE WORD.** It is about the Report, which is the same thing. From this you should know that nothing is an exception to anything. Everything is interwoven in one entity, since the SPIRIT is one and everything emanated from **ME THE SUPREME SPIRIT**. Therefore, *GO* and *COME*, is the same SPIRIT.

When you say, '*Go*' – the spirit brings out the energy, '*GO*' and when you say '*Come*', it is the same energy from the spirit, because where the '*Go*' came from is where the '*Come*' will go. That is the **SOURCE** and D**ESTINATION**. **Go**, is from the **SOURCE** and **Come** is from the **DESTINATION**. As you can see it became round, which is the circle, **GO** and **Come**.

If you '*STOP*' that is the middle, but it is either you **GO** or you **COME**. If you stop, you stop in the middle. So, **THE FATHER GOD** is '*GO*' – out and the **SON** is '*STOP*' – in the middle and the Holy Spirit is **COME**. So you see **Go, Go** and **Stop** and walk and **come** back to **go**. And then **go** and **come** back, that is, **go come**. And **Go, come, come go**. So, **stop** is the middle. That is the way it happens, **I** have made it clear '**GO' 'COME, 'COME GO, STOP** in the middle "**MANIFESTATION**". So that is the circle – the ring of the power of GOD **OOO**, which is the energy of Reports.

C: **WHO ARE REPORTERS**

These are the messengers that carry this information. As you are hearing this information you must report to one another – those who have not heard about this **INFORMATION.**

This has now stepped down to humans – man, the Reporter. What type of report do you give out to people? What type of information do you hear and you keep in your position. Why don't you keep quiet if it is negative? Why don't you speak out if it is positive?

Every human being on earth is a **Reporter.** Who gives you the things to report on? It is either God or Satan. It is either the Positive Instinct or Negative Instinct. It is either you hear good news or you hear bad news. When you open your mouth and say something you have made yourself a **Reporter.** This is introduction to this. You will hear more in the full Lecture Revelation.

D: THE WORD OF EVERLASTING RECORD

This **WORD** is the **WORD** of **Everlasting Record**. This is **THE TESTIMONY OF EVERLASTING GOSPEL** – The Last Witness about **THE FATHER GOD** on earth, which means that generation upon generations everybody – all human beings will talk about **FATHER GOD,**

Information

FATHER GOD, FATHER GOD, and FATHER TALK (GOD PRESENT). That is **MY** Aim and Objective of possessing His Royal Majesty King Solomon David ETE as **The Supreme Reporter of THE FATHER GOD'S SUPREME INFORMATION CENTRE** (THE INBUILT SPIRITUAL LIBRARY) **OF THE UNIVERSAL SUPREME WORD**.

You hear about the prophets of old like Isaiah, Isaac, Ezekiel, Abraham, David, Samuel and many others. All of them were Divine Reporters of God, but their information used to come through angels, because since **MY DIVINE SOUL, THE SUPREME WORD, THE CHRIST OF THE FATHER GOD, THE KING OF KINGS AND THE LORD OF LORDS** did not die and gave **ME THE FATHER GOD** the opportunity to come to mankind again as the **HOLY SPIRIT OF TRUTH**. Before then **I** was passing **MY** inspirations – **MY** instincts through angels – **MY** other Divine Selves, because the volume of the

Holy Spirit – the Supreme Light, human could not take and would not understand. Hence **I** use angels to pass information through to human being, because of that the spiritual wave was not very clear. They gave most of the information because of their stage of mind and also because of their lower stage of human beings. So, angels somehow did a bit of other things like needing small, small things – small sacrifices. Therefore, those angels will say bring candles, burn incense and bring some other things for them, before they deliver message. Before they do anything human must conducted some kind of rituals action, because humanity was deep in sins. Since, **MY SOUL** came into this world and used the Supreme blood, the Almighty Power of the blood of Christ wash human beings clean, this made **ME** have access direct to mankind now as it was in the beginning. Now **MY DIVINE SELF, THE HOLY SPIRIT OF TRUTH** is with mankind again has it been in the

Information

beginning of time when **I** first create Adam and Eve.

This is the reason many people are inspired in this world as **Reporters** of Good News of **THE FATHER GOD**. You can see them on television and all over the place. You can also hear them on the Radio. Some of them pretend and they are using some negative means, but those means are not the power of their inspiration. They use those means as a source of protection; they do not believe and have faith in **THE FATHER GOD** because of fear of death. Nonetheless, **I, THE FATHER GOD** inspire them for all the positive words they speak. So they are **Reporters.**

They are many types of Reporters. The negative reporters are they that are featuring negative news because of money and of evil in them. There are so many agents who are evil reporters. You will hear of them in this Lecture Revelation.

However, **THE WORD OF EVERLASTING RECORDS** will

present good **INFORMATION,** the positive **INFORMATION** and reveal all these things. So that as you have access to this information you can now check yourself, search your heart what type of template you are and the type of **Reporter** you are. That is the reason you see ***THE WORD OF EVERLASTING RECORDS, THE TESTIMONY OF EVERLASTING GOSPEL*** coming out now through KING SOLOMON SPIRITUAL LIBRARY OF THE FATHER GOD TO ALL HUMANITY.

This is **MY** RECORDS AND INFORMATION THAT SHALL STAY FOR ETERNITY, GENERATIONS AFTER GENERATIONS for all positive children of **THE FATHER GOD** to live with, and use it as their guide line of life.

E: **THIS IS GOOD NEWS TO ALL MANKIND**

This **INFORMATION CENTRE –** KING SOLOMON SPIRITUAL LIBRARY

Information

– THE WORD CITY OF GOD is the **Good News for Mankind.** After **I** have finished the recreation of the universe and **I** make everything new spiritually, this is the very last thing to do. This is an earmark last record of **MY DIVINE SELF**, humankind dose not know that **THE FATHER GOD** is the Energy of life – the Supreme Soul, the **WORD.** That is what **I** refer to be the Christ of **THE FATHER GOD**, the Son of God. That Supreme Holy Spirit is the **WORD. HE** is everything of everything. So now **I** have revealed **MYSELF** to all mankind on earth.

STUDY THIS PROPERLY.
DO NOT THROW THIS INFORMATION AWAY.
DO NOT IGNORE IT EITHER. There is nobody on this earth if you are a living soul that should ignore this **INFORMATION CENTRE -** this **EVERLASTING RECORD.** Whether you call yourself a person of God or that of Satan, it does not matter, since you speak, reason very

carefully. Do not throw something that is good away. Do not allow Satan to make you ignore this message, because when you ignore this you will miss something that is far, far more than gold.

The Good News that you are hearing now – the Good Record – this **INFORMATION** from **THE INFORMATION CENTRE** is more than gold. This will be in the heart of every soul for eternity. Therefore **I AM** giving this **SUPREME INFORMATION** to mankind today. It is Good News – Total Good News for every soul in Heaven, on earth and all the planets for generations upon Generations to come, in million, trillion, and bringslion years, even life everlasting. This is **EVERLASTING RECORD.**

F: **BLESSED ARE THOSE WHO WILL USE THIS INFORMATION AND CHANGE THE WORLD**

This **INFORMATION** – this **FATHER'S TALK** of **GOD PRESENT** – this **SUPREME WORD** from **THE SUPREME WORD OF THE UNIVERSE, THE WORD HIMSELF** from **THE WORD CITY OF GOD** is the Good News to Mankind. Blessed are those who will use all this **INFORMATION** and all these things **I** pass through His Royal Majesty King Solomon David Jesse ETE, which is **MYSELF -GOD PRESENT** in Him, to change the world.

The world will not change by magic. No human being can change the world except **MY WORD**. Nonetheless, the instrument of great change is this news - this **INFORMATION.** Forget about the mundane information you have. This **INFORMATION** is to inspire your other positive information that you already have.

This **INFORMATION** is not to drive away what you know previously unless it is negative. It is to stamp what you already know. Sometimes **I,**

Information

THE FATHER GOD inspire people to speak the words in their preaching and the advice they give. Some people say they do not believe in God, but they speak well of the words of positive, that is God, more than even those who profess to believe in God. As long as you believe in the **WORD,** and as long as you use the **WORD,** you are with **THE FATHER GOD, THE SUPREME WORD OF THE UNIVERSE,** therefore, it does not matter. It is the concept of misunderstanding when people say God or Satan or this or that. Nevertheless, the evil words, the negative word are Satan while the positive words are God. Therefore, God means good and good means **THE FATHER GOD.** Therefore blessed are you or any soul that use any form of Good Information to change the world. The starting point is from your own very self. Then your family, village, town, then community, and then the Nation, and certainly the whole world will then change for good.

You cannot use guns and bullets, bombs or evil practices or killings to change the world. You can only use this **LIGHT – THE SUPREME LIGHT OF THE UNIVERSE, THE PRACTICAL WORD** to change the world. Stand in this LIGHT – this Truth, and then you change the world for good.

I AM making everything possible for this **WORD** to come to pass – for this **INFORMATION** to come out, to establish this in the world at last. Before **I** establish this, **I** passed through a lot of things. Since **I AM Here – I AM everywhere, Here and There** and **I put MY** feet down with **MY Supreme Energy of Love** and conquered all manners of negativism and bring out this **WORD – THE SUPREME LIGHT OF THE UNIVERSE – THE SUPREME INFORMATION.** Use this **information - THE SUPREME WORD** which shall inspire you now. It will inspire all ages of people. This **SUPREME WORD** will inspire people of all ages and every age group.

All the works and all the business you do, this word will inspire you to do more in a positive mode.

Obviously a lot of people have accessed King Solomon's previous preaching like in Ecclesiastic, Song of Solomon, Proverbs, Psalms and many other things – from the Holy Bible are all inspirational. And as a matter of fact, inclusive are also the words inspired by you.

Every good thought brings good words. Every good word brings good hearing. Every good hearing brings good practice. So think well, speak well so that the people hear well and then they can do well. With thinking well, speaking well and hearing well doing well will be possible on earth. And this is the **INFORMATION** you will use.

Importantly, **I THE SUPREME WORD OF THE UNIVERSE** now

attached **MY SOUL** to His Royal Majesty King Solomon David Jesse ETE to establish KING SOLOMON SPIRITUAL LIBRARY - GOD UNIVERSAL INFORMATION CENTRE physically here on earth so that every word that is processed here is based on positivism. There is no mixture here. That does not mean that **I** only pass through Him to speak.

Nonetheless if you heard this **WORD** and removed your ears from it that means you are not correct, because every correct child must always link to his or her father.

If therefore, you are not linked to this **INFORMATION** ask yourself second thought – where is your information coming from? Who is inspiring you?

Because all positives things are from one place and all negative things are from one place. Unless you are pretending by doing negative and pretentiously presenting it like positive, then you will hate this information. However, if you are positive in everything you are doing this information is acting as a Father, as a background of all positive information on earth. So, blessed are those who will use this information and change the whole world.

Change yourself.

Change your family.

Change the children even yet to born million and million years to come.

Change the whole world.

Make everywhere good including the governments, churches and indeed everywhere and everything. Use this as a guide in everything that you do.

Before you comment on any of **THE FATHER'S TALK**, make sure you read at least seven **FATHER'S TALK.** Read at least Seven **FATHER'S TALK GOD PRESENT** completely, before you can make any comment. If you do not read complete seven **FATHER'S TALK GOD PRESENT** that cover the Seven

Spirits of God from Adam day, first day of the week to Christ Our Lord day, the seventh day of the week, then do not make any comment to go into conclusion about the **FATHER'S TALK** INFORMATION, because you will make silly mistakes to your soul.

Make sure you have seven titles different **FATHER'S TALK** and read them completely. Study them and understand them before you make any comment.

G: **I AM THE SUPREME INTRODUCER OF LIFE**

I, THE SUPREME WORD OF THE UNIVERSE, THE CREATOR OF HEAVEN AND EARTH, THE FATHER GOD, I AM THE SUPREME INTRODUCER OF LIFE. Anything **I** have not introduced can never come to pass. Nobody will hear. Nobody will know. **I AM** the ONE that introduces everything in different stages, from un-hear able, unseen able and untouchable to hear able, seen able and touchable by the **SUPREME WORD**. Therefore, **I** have now introduced this **MY SUPREME AND DIVINE INFORMATION CENTRE** to all mankind.

If you do anything via the word, whether it is profitable business for money or just as a good gesture or for hearing or for education and you expect people to believe you, why don't you believe this one? If you do believe this Word then everything will be well with you now and even next time of your life on earth.

Know it today that **I AM The Supreme Introducer of Life** and **I AM** introducing a completely new life - life elevation on earth. So, THIS IS THE MANUAL FOR ALL **REPORTERS,** all human beings, all companies and all governments. Everybody that uses the word should read this **INFORMATION** so that you know where you stand for that is, the type of spirit you are dealing with. Where is your information coming from?

Information

Where do you store your information?

What do you believe in?

What do you do and via what?

It is via the **SUPREME WORD OF THE UNIVERSE.**

INFORMATION

PART TWO:
INFORMATION

A: **WHAT IS INFORMATION?**

B: **THE SUPREME INTELLIGENT SPIRIT GEN**

C: **THE GENESIS OF ALL THINGS**

D: **THE BUBBLE OF CREATION**

E: **THE SERVANT OF THE WORD IS INFORMATION**

F: **WHY THE WORD LIVES IN EVERY PERSON**

G: **MAN IS A DISTRIBUTION CENTRE FOR ALL TYPE OF INFORMATION**

The above are the sub-titles that cover Part Two – **INFORMATION.**

A: **WHAT IS INFORMATION?**

As **I** said earlier, **INFORMATION** is already explained. Everybody knows the meaning of **INFORMATION.** It is the Centre of Self. You can call it spirit, wherever the **WORD** is kept. Wherever news is gathered is **INFORMATION CENTRE,** but **INFORMATION** itself is the **WORD –** the hearing, the events – what is happening.

When **I, THE SUPREME WORD** cause something to happen, **I** want to hear what is happening. That is the meaning of **INFORMATION.** That is what **I** call testimony. This **WORD** is **INFORMATION.** The hearing of it is the actual meaning of **INFORMATION.**

INFORMATION itself is event that was caused by the **WORD.**

INFORMATION of the Silent Thought is the **WORD.**

INFORMATION of the **WORD** is the events that occurred.

When events come to pass then there will be information about it – the news about it - the good news about it. In other words the Bible is called good news. That means it is INFORMATION. This **FATHER'S TALK (**GOD PRESENT**)** is good news, new records. That is **INFORMATION.** That is the actual meaning of **THE FATHER'S TALK GOD PRESENT.**

King Solomon Spiritual Library means **INFORMATION CENTRE.** What is the **INFORMATION?** The **INFORMATION** consists of different types of the titled Lectures Revelations as you are hearing now. Those are the **INFORMATION** itself.

So, this is **THE FATHER GOD.** This is the **WORD.** This is the totality of everything together.

You do not need to ask questions again. You don't need anyone to interpret anything for you again. If somebody has to interpret this **INFORMATION** – this **FATHER'S TALK** for you it has to be for language reasons. Whatever your language and dialect, this **INFORMATION** must be interpreted into that for you to gain better understanding of the **WORD** – the meaning of the **WORD** or that language. It is not to interpret the actual **INFORMATION,** because this is Lecture Revelation.

I brought this Lecture Revelation and presented in a way that you do not need an interpreter to gain the knowledge. What you are hearing is exactly what **I** mean and what it is. Nonetheless, somebody can be inspired through this, to help give this **INFORMATION** to the whole world.

B: **THE SUPREME INTELLIGENT SPIRIT GEN**

The **INFORMATION** is the Supreme Intelligent Spirit *GEN*, which is **MY** soul. Before the sound came to manifest, the first energy **I** created into Adam is the spirit Gen. **I** was on top of the water generating this energy to formulate sound – heee – heer, heee – heer, heee – heer – father – mother, father – mother, father – mother; male – female.

Then, when the speed went higher than normal, it became chi-chi-chi-chi-chi-chi-chi-chi-chi-chi –gha-gha-gha-gha-gha. Then that speed tuned the sound from heee-heer to ha-ha-ha-ha-wah-wah-wah-wah. And that is what you see when a child breathes as soon as the child is born, the baby starts to cry in a loud voice. That is the **GEN** telling people 'I have arrived!'

What actually makes a human being to be a human being starting from the stage hen in the mother's womb is this component called **GEN.**

GEN is an amplifier of the **WORD** that is born. This is what a woman actually takes in from a man's system. The man passes the **GEN** into the woman and that is the bubble of nature – bubble of life. When this **GEN** goes into the woman's incubator that is, the woman's womb, it develops. As soon as that **GEN** is given birth to, it proved himself or herself as God's house that the amplifier of the **WORD** is in that house. That means God is living in that child. Hence a child cries at birth. It is an announcement. But the cry will not be meaningful. Nonetheless, the energy of life will be kicking and speaking. That sound is the **GEN of LIFE** – that is Genesis of everything in the physical life, from **GEN** to Genesis and from Genesis to Generator of Life. That is about the **MY Supreme Intelligent Spirit** called **GEN. I, THE FATHER GOD AM ALL AND ALL**, I motivated the component call **GEN** in every human being as soul energy of the spoken **WORD**, so that at the end of it all **INFORMATION** will come out as **THE WORD**.

Information

The **GEN** operates through the hyphen of the tongue before the words can come out from human's mouth, without that you will be thinking, but you can't speak. So the act of speaking is the thought and when the speaking manifest **THE WORD** via the **GEN,** then you can hear what the **WORD** talks, just as you are hearing this Lecture Revelation **INFORMATION.**

C: **THE GENESIS OF ALL THINGS**

This is the Genesis of all things; **I AM THE FATHER GOD – THE SPIRIT** revealing this **GOOD NEWS OF INFORMATION** to you means that **I AM** giving you something more that **GOLD** in the heart of every human that is alive. Even if you think you are a negative person in this generation and you accepted this **INFORMATION,** you should take voluntary evolution to positivism next time you come on earth. Wish yourself to be good coming back on earth through this great news of **THE FATHER GOD**.

Start immediately to think well about this **INFORMATION.** Speak well about this **INFORMATION.** Let people hear well about this **INFORMATION**. The good action will start to yield from your input into your own inner self.

This Component **GEN** is called the Inner Shrine in every human. It came out from one entity, **THE FATHER GOD – HE IS THE SPIRIT** that manifested the **WORD –** the sound as **SUPREME ECHO OF LIFE**.

So with this type of **INFORMATION,** this has never been released before in this magnitude with Potency of Everlasting Energy of God.

It is more than any protection.

This **INFORMATION** alone protects your life.

It solves all your problems.

It makes you whole in spirit, in soul and in the physical life.

When you believe this **INFORMATION,** you believe in **THE**

SUPREME WORD OF THE UNIVERSE, the Creator of Heaven and Earth, the one that everybody tap from all ideas through **WORD** doing all sorts of things and deceive you, and makes money. But if attach yourself to this Centre – this Information you are hearing now you attach yourself to the Supreme Unlimited Memory, Unlimited Power, Unlimited Energy that guides you and protects you. Believe in it, it is more than anything. You do not need to keep any objects, just believe this **WORD.** Drink this idea- this **INFORMATION** into your system and you are fit in all capacities, in your spirit, soul and physical truth. That is **The Genesis Of All Things – the INFORMATION HIMSELF – HE IS THE SPIRIT, HE IS THE WORD** and man is the House of the **WORD** where you are hearing this **INFORMATION – the TRINITY FATHER GOD.**

D: **THE BUBBLE OF CREATIONS**

Through this **GEN**, this power, this idea **I** generated the **Bubble of Creation - *LET* this and that happen.** So, the Bubble of Creation for all types and capacities of creations came from **MY** Inner Shrine – **MY** Inner Soul via **GEN** the Spoken Word, the idea and the thought before the pronouncements is making.

The force that came out from **MY** Inner Shrine – **MY** inner Self-Soul that force voiced, the pronouncements is attached to the Supreme Energy that makes things happen. This is profound knowledge, which you should believe. It is more than any secret society knowledge in this world. This is an Open Nation – an Open Universe – an Open Word of **THE FATHER GOD**.

E: **THE SERVANT OF THE WORD IS INFORMATION**

The Servant of **THE FATHER GOD – HE IS THE SPIRIT** is the **WORD.**

The **WORD** manifests **THE FATHER GOD'S** mind. The **WORD** manifests the thoughts of **THE FATHER GOD**. The Supreme thought of **GOD** – the Supreme Mind of **GOD** manifest through the **WORD.** That is why the **WORD** is the Son of God, but **HE, THE WORD** is also **GOD HIMSELF.** The Son of **THE FATHER GOD** is **GOD**.

What you call **GOD** is **the WORD.** What you call **THE FATHER GOD** is **HE IS THE SPIRIT** that motivates the **WORD.** And now the **WORD HIMSELF** is causing something to happen. Then the News of the event is this **INFORMATION.** It is the Servant of the **WORD.**

F: **WHY THE WORD LIVES IN EVERY PERSON**

Ask yourself this question, why does the **WORD** live in you? The reason the **WORD** lives in every person is to manifest the **INFORMATION,** to show that **I** the SPIRIT lives in **THE WORD** and **THE WORD** lives in man, and man also lives in the universe, lives in the atmosphere, *live life*. That means it is round – in a circle **OOO**.

THE SPIRIT lives in the **WORD,** the **WORD** lives in man and man also lives in spirit – the atmosphere, in the womb of the earth, which is **THE SPIRIT** also, which is **THE FATHER GOD.** So, it is from SOURCE to DESTINATION and DESTINATION to the SOURCE. That is the reason you see **OOO**.

You cannot do anything reasonable and meaningful as this **INFORMATION** and take away the concept of three rings - **OOO** in entity that is, the spirit, the soul and physical. You cannot and if you do not understand, you should understand now. That is the reason negativism, which is the pretending energy does

Information

not like to hear about that entity – the Supreme three rings the letters **OOO**, because when **OOO** arrive the good ideas, the good information, the positive information comes and every other information is dismissed.

You access stories to know the truth. Since the truth came all stories ceased, all negative evil information ceased automatically when **THE SUPER HOLY INFORMATION GOOD NEWS** arrived. You can upgrade your knowledge with this information.

Every human being that is correct, positive and being honest to his or her self should try and read seven **FATHER'S TALK GOD PRESENT** from King Solomon Spiritual Library. When you have finished studying them, then you have decisions to make for yourself. Either you are positive or negative. That is the order "**OBEYGO**". Try it and see.

There is nothing wrong in knowing about something before you decide on how to deal with that thing. If you

Information

dismiss something before you know what it is, you make a great mistake, and you are not a truthful person. What will you say, if you are asked, "***did you actually asked questions***?" Did you ask to know?

Okay, you want to travel from Nigeria to London, but it happened that you are not at Lagos Airport, but you are at Ghana Airport or Cotonou Airport or Cameroon Airport or indeed any of the other African Airports. Then you refused to board the plane there, where you are with the reason that you are not in Lagos or Abuja or in any particular Airport in Nigeria. How do you know that all Airports are not linked to Lagos or Heathrow or Gatwick Airport? You dismissed that. How would you then know? Check well before you refused to board your flight that tells you that they are taking you to London. It is stupidity and lack of understanding to refuse things you do not know yet whether is positive or negative.

Information

A mad man begging for money said to a servant of God, 'Give me money! Give me money!' The servant of God put hand in his pocket and brought out twenty-naira note and gave to the mad man. The mad man said no, 'I want money.'

He brought out fifty-naira note and gave to the mad man. The mad man refused. He brought out a hundred-naira note. The mad man said he did not want that one. The servant of God brought out all the big, big notes of money and offered him. The mad man refused all of them. The servant of God even offered a fifty-pound note to the mad man, he still refused. Frustrated he asked the mad man what it was he really wanted. The mad man replied, 'I want money!' The man of God was confused.

In truth mad people do not know what they are looking for. After sometime the mad man asked another person to give him money. The man dipped hand in his pocket and brought out ten kobo coin and gave to the mad person. The mad man collected and said, 'thank you, yes you have given me the money.'

The man of God was still around and saw that and exclaimed oh - ho! So this is the money the mad man was looking for! That is only ten kobo. Ten kobo would not buy anything in Nigeria, let alone anywhere else in the world. It was just like ten pence or ten cents. Yet the mad man happily took that refusing all the big notes he was offered.

The man of God could not explain to the mad man that the ten kobo was not good money even though it was money since it would not get him anything.

So, you will never understand that the wisdom and the knowledge you claim to have will not lead you to anywhere until you understand that money does not consist of only coins. You can make one million notes in money. Just one note and it is one million. You can carry that one to anywhere. That is what is termed the real money and it is easy to carry.

So you see, since you have arrogance, since you think you are a preacher, since you think you are a Governor, a President, a Head of State, you are highly spiritual – you claim all sorts of things. You study this and study that and have Masters Degree and PhD. That blinded you from something better in front of you. If, however, you keep them aside and look for something more fulfilling than the transient things, you will become aware of your blindness.

Get any information no matter how odd it looked and read them. Such information could be paraded that it is Satan's Information. Get closer to it to ascertain the truth. You may find out that they labelled it to be Satan's Information, but the actual energy – the actual Information does not present Satan.

In the same token you could even hear the one they say God Information. They boldly display **JEHOVAH GOD, JESUS, and EMMANUEL, ELOHIM, LOVE –** and all sorts of other names. You saw that and concluded that you have come across God's people and you went inside and they cut-off your head, because they practiced evil and not the true word of God. It could be satanic practice going on there. Do not judge from what you heard, judge from what you know and what you witnessed.

This **INFORMATION** came about so that any correct human being, whether you are leader of a church, a King, a Queen, a President and so on, should not hear news and take action. Find out the truth about what you heard, if not so, you are looking to get a bag with coins of money rather than obtaining the one with the bank notes with huge monetary value.

Information

You have inadvertently refused to attach yourself to many positive people, because Satan came to tell you that that man is not good, that woman is not good, and they are coming to take your position.

Do you know what evil do? In this Lecture Revelation you will know that evil tendency is to give you bad news, bad information to barrier you from all good things. And before you know it is too late.

I give you a husband or a wife that is good for you. Somebody who hates you would say that your husband or your wife is a womaniser or a prostitute. I caught him with another woman or her with a man. When you miss that man or that woman, all that comes to you are evil, womaniser and prostitutes themselves will now come to you because that is what Satan provided for you after successfully taking away your good partner. So, be careful with information you receive and action you take.

The reason the **WORD** lives in every person is that you should have the ability by yourself to know the truth before you judge. **I** don't make anybody a slave, where life or the Spoken Word or Thought is concerned. Everybody has **THOUGHT**.

Everybody SPEAK **WORD**.

Everybody is a **HUMAN PERSON**.

You are a person and you are independently in **THE FATHER GOD**. King Solomon is as an independent Human God. He is not answerable to anybody. Everybody is answerable to one thing and that is **THE WORD,** the Conscience *THE SUPREME CONSCIENCE*.

With this **GOOD NEWS** of **INFORMATION, I AM** now liberated everybody soul; everybody on earth is liberated, whether you are an adult or a child. You the child is liberated does not mean you should not be respectful and also that you should not take instructions from the elders. A child that takes orders and instructions from the parents as respect to their parents does not mean that the parents have rights to control the child. The husband that gives orders to his wife with her respectfully obliging does not mean you have right to control your wife. These responses are for love, ordinance, and good arrangement and for peaceful co-existence. That does not mean the person cannot decide to leave you, if she wanted to. You cannot enslave the **WORD.**

   I in everybody made everybody independent person in all capacities. That is the reason **I** established Human Rights on earth. Nonetheless, the truth is that everybody is enslaved to the Truth, which is the actual fact of every situation. So, when you know the truth you should be a slave to that truth and that set you free.

   When therefore, you do not know the true position of anything and you take action or make a decision based on that or accept it, then you are a slave to that untrue position. Then you are not God – you are not good. Your judgement and decision is wrong.

Be careful about receiving reports and information from people that works for you or are under you. That is the reason the **WORD** lives in every person. It makes you independent. It makes you autonomous, which is having the freedom to make decisions and act independently.

G: **HUMAN IS A DISTRIBUTION CENTRE FOR ALL KIND OF INFORMATION**

Every person is a Distribution Centre, but what type of information is stored in you? Is it positive information? Or is it negative information? Who is working for you? Who brings news to you? Your wife, is she positive to you? Your child, is she or he supporting you? Or are you a positive person?

Check around you. Check around your organization, your company, your country, your cabinets and your workers. Whoever that works for you, what information do they kneel down or stand up or sit down or dream-up to tell you, and you took action based on that? Do you know their minds whether they formulated the information they feeding you with?

They could say it was a dream they had. They could profess to have seen with their own eyes. They could do anything at all. Read **THE FATHER'S TALK** Lecture Revelation titled **BEWARES** and another titled **POST, POSITION AND NAME**. When you are done in reading them draw understanding from all of them and put them together, then your eyes will surely open.

You will know that in this world you are independent person. **I AM THE FATHER GOD** in you can make you to understand things better than what you know today or before.

Since the mad man thought that the only money consist of coins, he does not believe that there is paper notes of money. He refused even the fifty-pound note and rather took the ten-coin money, which is equal to nothing. That is exactly what you will do with **THE FATHER'S TALK** Lectures Revelation if you are evil and not careful. 'Oh I am a preacher. I am a Head of State. I am a Queen. I am a King. I am a Prime Minister. I went to School. I am a leader of the church, I am the leader, I am an ardent preacher and a healer, I am a visionary, I am a Child of God, I am this I am that.' All are NONSENSE ALTOGETHER!

If you are all that in reality then listen to this **INFORMATION** read seven **FATHER'S TALK GOD PRESENT** then you justify your conscience. Without that you are receiving coins instead of the higher money in higher value.

INFORMATION

PART THREE
REPORT

A: **WHAT IS REPORT**

B: **INFORMATION ALSO MEANS REPORT**

C: **AN OFFICIAL REPORT**

D: **NON-OFFICIAL REPORT**

E: **EVIL PEOPLE LIKE REPORT**

F: **THE SIGN OF A GOOD LEADER**

G: **DO NOT NEED A REPORT FROM HUMANS IF YOU ARE A GOOD LEADER**

Those are the sub-titles that comprise the Part Three of this Lecture Revelation **INFORMATION**.

A: **WHAT IS A REPORT?**

A **Report** as **I** said earlier is the actual news of the **INFORMATION** of events.

Maybe if you read this **INFORMATION** in the view that **I AM** the same **WORD** will make you to understand more, because **I AM** the inspiration. This WORD - this Lecture Revelation - this spirit of **INFORMATION** is inspiration. While you are reading and accepting this, **I** will be in you to give you more insight, because **I AM** unlimited memory. The **WORD** is **Unlimited Phenomenon.** So, no mouth can explain every **WORD** about every **WORD**.

Every **WORD** continues to be every **WORD,** and meaningful continues to be deeply meaningful. For that reason, do not think that when you are reading **THE FATHER'S TALK GOD PRESENT,** that I have put everything down.

Every **FATHER'S TALK GOD PRESENT** is coded with a spiritual key. When you read one of the key **WORD**, immediately inside your heart, **I The Supreme Thought** in you will activate **MYSELF** in you and then give you deeper meaning and understanding in a positive way than what this paper can contain. So, for that you are linked to **ME** through **THE FATHER'S TALK (GOD PRESENT)** through this **INFORMATION.**

More information will unveil inside of you via the Supreme Thought of God in you if you are positive. And even if you are negative the same thing will occur. You will be liberated inside of your mind. Therefore, this is the **REPORT, THE INFORMATION I AM** making today directly to your soul.

The **Report I AM** making is that in **MY** own record **I** see human beings taking so many reports from side talks. They listen to people negatives reports instead of listening to **ME the Holy Spirit of Truth**.

Satan use reports a lot, than any other spirit soul in human beings , because when somebody has no access to somebody what they have is reliant on reports.

Before armed robbers strike somewhere they'll need information about where they are going to carry out operations. All the criminals, evil practices, evil spirits anything they do, require report. Without report they cannot do it. That is the reason the more you talk, the more you explain yourself and the more you become open.

As **I AM talking-talking** now, **I** make **MYSELF** known to the whole world. Prior to now you did not know. Previously people ponder over God and wondering what this God is, what is the Father, what is Christ, what is King and what is Servant, what is Christianity, what are Muslim and what religion is, now you know that all means one and only one thing **THE UNIVERSAL SUPREME WORD, THE GOOD NEWS, THE INFORMATION**. Matter of fact the reason a lot of people say they do not believe in God is because they are not able to know the meaning of God, but what about good?

What about love?
What about mercy?
What about kindness?
What about equality?
What about righteousness - honesty?

Righteousness means honesty in everything you do. All that means God, they mean good, well, nice, and fine. What do they all mean? They mean Good God.

So, what do death, poverty, problems, sickness, hatred, envy, strife, jealousy and tribalism and all the rest of the bad ideas mean? They all mean Satan. All bad ideas and bad words mean Satan.

How many people like to be envied – really badly?

How many people like people to be jealous of them? How many people like people to kill them?

How many people like others to tell lies about them? How many people like to be discriminated against?

How many people like people to be pompous and arrogant before them?

Since you do not like those things, it automatically means you hate Satan. This is the meaning of it.

Therefore, do not go to condemn people and say this person does not know God. Do you know the meaning of God? May be you do not even know who is **THE FATHER GOD ALMIGHTY**, you who go to tell people that they do not come to church, they do not know **THE FATHER GOD**, they do not believe **THE FATHER GOD.** You who go to church and tell lies and hate people, gang up against people, destroy people's character, do you know God, then talking about knowing **THE FATHER GOD**? Do you know **THE FATHER GOD?** You who judge based on one side – without hearing from the other side, do you know **THE FATHER GOD?**

People reckon God judge according to what he hears. That is a lie! Which GOD? God judge according to what **HE** hears. **I, THE FATHER GOD, THE SUPREME JUDGE OF THE UNIVERSE I,** hear before you speak because **I AM** in your heart. So, what **I** know, see and hear from every individual is what **I** judge. This is unlike what you hear because someone could speak differently from what they have in mind and you judge according to what you hear and you hate your soul. So, from today, if you have access to this **INFORMATION** never take anybody's report to judge someone unless you hear from both side and the person reported to you.

A good judge would make sure that the person confessed. Even when you torture someone so much then the person would confess, is wrong. You can make someone to plead guilty when they are not guilty, because the torture is too much. That is the reason if read the Lecture Revelation titled **NATURAL** you will know that everything **I** do, **I** done them in a natural way. When you get the facts of a situation, then you can give a good judgement.

    I hear and **I** see and **I** know – in three capacities, before **I** pass judgement. What **I** hear – because **I** live in every thought; what **I** see – because the **WORD** manifest what **I** see and what **I** know – because **I AM THE FATHER GOD** who created you, **I** know before you do. That is how **MY** judgement is true. You who want to judge people would you know that from anybody?

    As a matter of fact, His Royal Majesty King Solomon David Jesse ETE, no human being knows Him on this earth except **THE FATHER GOD** alone. So, how can you judge someone like that? Are you going to judge Him, because of his food or because of how He dresses or because of how He looks like? Is that how you are going to judge Him? What about His capacity and what He stands for?

There was someone called Reverend Mkpanam in Calabar. **I** created that man nature and buried the spirit soul inside him called '**Rich-am**'. The man lived and died and nobody decoded that **RICHNESS NATURE** in him. So he went back with the blessing. Nobody knew that Reverend Mkpanam was the actual 'Riches'. It was that if you attached to him you became rich. Every human being on earth is like that.

When you talk about Nation, it is human being. When you talk about country, it is human being. When you talk about love, it is human being, so also peace. Every component of good natures is buried in human beings. The same thing is applicable with negative components. They are equally buried in humans. So, if you attach with goodness, you tap the components of goodness in people.

If you love one another then the goodness of everybody will be revealed to you and then you exchange it for good. That is the reason love is the answer.

That is the meaning of - **What Is Report.** Be careful with the type of **Report** you receive because Satan wants the news. Have you seen what the Reporter of News in the whole world does?

B: **INFORMATION ALSO MEANS REPORT**

The same thing happens here as with the **Reports** above. The ideas with which people say things from what they thought or what they heard or what they saw.

There are three types of **INFORMATION Report** that people hear. One is thinking – imagination.

Information

One is hearing it, including, hearsay. One is seeing it, witnessing it, and knowing it that it is the truth.

So, what you say to **ME** or what you say to somebody who is your father, your mother, the leader of your church, your preacher, your King, your manager, your higher officer, to use it against somebody, did you hear them yourself? Did you think and making them up yourself? Did you see or witnessed the event you are reporting? How did you manage to know the **Information** that you released about them, to be used in a negative manner or even positive manner against someone?

Different countries have their spies known as secret agents that go about digging **Information** from other places. How can you trust that person you trained when you are not sure he or she has not been bribed? How are you sure the spy or agent is providing the right information to the nation.

Think about it. Think very well about this Lecture Revelation.
Without this Lecture Revelation and doing things correctly you will not have peace in this world, because when you make a mistake it follows you forever.

    I send a lot of people to this world to lead the church, to lead organization, because you say you are truthful; because you say you love. **I** inspire with the Holy Spirit, but when Satan comes and give you wrong information, you use that to spoil a lot of things. Even in the Kingdom of God, wrong information spoils things. You can be Satan when you live by information instead of being God. The reason is that the information you are hearing from, do you know whether it is Imagination Information – he or she think. Or do you know whether the information that is given to you was obtained second hand? Again, do you know whether the information that was brought to you was an eyewitness account and it is true? Which of them will convince you that that is the correct information? **I** will give a story:

There was a big person –
I *do not want to mention the name, who has so many servant and would send them out as preachers or agents to help people to expand the mission or organization.*

There was a man that was so clever and due to his cleverness and humility, everybody was always afraid being around him. He was so honest that everything he saw and heard he would advice himself about that and would start to kick against it if it bothered the organization because he loved the organization and he loves his master. So everybody around this man was careful whenever they saw him.

He became a threat to the baddies in the community and all the evil people. Unless you are positive and truthful then you would like him.

From the way he talks and the way he lives his life people knew him as an open and honest person. So, one day they ganged up and went to their master with a tale that this thing that this other person was accused of there is no truth about it.

Then one of them asked to confirm with the master about two certain people and what was wrong with them? And then the master asked them what their problem was. They said, 'oh master I thought that the information you asked of me – that news that you heard and asked me, I thought that your servant is the one that gave you the information.

You see that he was thinking it was that open and honest servant that reported the matter to the Master. While in actual fact, this servant has never for one day knelt down one day before the Master to report a single soul to him in this life. And he will never do that. He has no time for that.

This is honest, quiet and humble servant to the master and because of that action that person was done for.

When you gang up against a truthful person you are finished.

I, THE FATHER GOD lives in everybody. **I** do not allow judgement by humans. Humans will always take sides. Every human being is likely to take sides. **THE FATHER GOD** alone does not take sides. **HE** lives in everybody's heart and knows the truth about every human. What the person stands for. What they can do and what they cannot do. So God's judgement alone – **THE FATHER GOD'S** alone is the true judgement. You shall see in this world. The truth shall come to pass.

Let people desert you. Let people despise you. Let people disown you. Have patience when the truth arrives you will be one of the town, one of the universe, one of the whole nation because of the truth.

Hold fast onto the truth. Be yourself, stand where you are. Represent what you represent. The truth shall come out at last.

That is why **I** said that **INFORMATION** also means **Report**. But be careful regarding the kind of **Report** you are giving out and the kind of **Report** you are receiving.

C: AN OFFICIAL REPORT

The meaning of an official report is that when you send somebody on an errand or to perform a duty, the person should give a report to that effect. That is not the type of **Report I** said you should not receive.

Even that official report, did the reporter give you true report? It could be that there was a gang up to give you a bad report. You have to know the truth about these things, because an official report could be falsified.

The reporter could personally decide to give a bad report. That sort of report because it is official, the reporter therefore is authorised to talk to you. That is what is termed **Official Report. Official Reporter** is someone that is entitled to speak.

I, THE FATHER GOD sends out angels. **I** know everything. **I AM THE WORD. I AM THE THOUGHT** but **I** also send angels to witness things. Man also witnesses things. So **I** have all capacities of receiving **Reports.** The ones **I** know. The ones **I** hear. The one **I** see before **I** pass judgement. **I** do not pass judgement as humans.

What do humans know?

Do you live in everybody's heart?

Are you activated in everybody's soul?

Are you the Atmosphere?

Are you The Supreme Thought?

How can you then judge? Out of one million cases you judge maybe none is true judgement. That is what happens in this world. And that is the reason there are problems.

If you misjudge somebody because of Report, from that day you become evil. So you have to be very careful.

From today, if you know that you have judged somebody wrongly – you passed judgement, you imagined something about someone wrongly about any situation or anything, reverse it immediately you hear this information and correct yourself.

If you speak evil about someone or something you do not know, go and make sure that you are correct with your assumption. If not then that is your downfall. This is the only way you can correct your situation – through this **INFORMATION.** Since you are alive to hear this News you have opportunity to take evolution away from evil that Satan uses bad reports, gossips and all sorts of things, including strife and jealousy to spread bad news in the whole world and causing problems and restlessness all over the world. Politicians suffer the most as a result of bad reports because when Satan knows that you are doing politics, even in Heaven, he will use you and capitalize on it.

When people know that you like Reports to use to judge and that you like to believe them, they would go about giving you more and more wrong information. As a result you will continue to fail in your business.

So an **OFFICIAL REPORT** is the report you authorise someone to tell you. Some people authorise someone to hide somewhere and listen to people's talk that is, eavesdropping. Some others send people as spies to countries, companies, organizations and even individuals because you have evil plan against the people you are spying on. Or it could be that you have good plan about the people you are spying.

Before you want to do something good for a person, you need a good report about that person. You will need a true report – a true position of that person. Before you can invest on somebody you need to know the true position of that person. You will require good information from that source.

Therefore, **INFORMATION** works for good or for bad but be careful if it is official.

D: NON-OFFICIAL REPORT

Non-Official Report is **INFORMATION** that people give you through busybody, gossips, jealousy, strife, envy. Somebody comes to you and say – I have something to tell you. And you asked what that was and the person tells you. Listen to what the person had to tell you. If it turned out that the person brought a bad report about somebody, damn the person there and then. Rebuke the person instantly! The person will never come back to give such reports.

If, however, you kept quiet and then acted on the information the person gave you and the person got wind of it, maybe you sacked someone based on that information, the person will be happy and thank Satan. Next time the person plans for another victim. That is why there are problems in the family, in churches, in the workplace and many other places.

What did Judas Iscariot use to betray Our Lord Jesus Christ? Everybody that is evil use bad reports, formulated report, gang-up report, jealousy, strife, pomposity, arrogance, gossip – all that is what evil use as **information and Report** to spoil relationships.

Therefore, if you want to be a nice person, if you want good people to be around you, do not listen to gossips; do not take people's report and judge. If you do you will miss all positive people around you. The ones that will be with you are the evil people. Those are the ones that forced their way to

Information

hang around you because you give them that chance. Those are the people that use **Non-Official Reports.**

If you did not send someone to bring report to you, damn the person if they do, 'did I send you for any information?' Is the appropriate question to ask the person, which means the person is a gossiper. The person that gave you good report can also give you bad report. Be careful. Never let the person know that you took their report and judge.

E: **EVIL PEOPLE LIKE REPORT**

Satanic agents – the evil people are those that like **Reports** too much because that is what they use to condemn people and to plan evil.

Godly people know things and they believe in things but they do not use **Reports** to judge people. So, what type of **Report** are you using? Is it **Official Report or Non-Official Report, Busybody Report?**

Information

A woman gives a man report about another woman and you think she has not fallen in love with you? You think any woman that wants you will talk good about another woman you are in love with?

You think people seeing you as a star and as a prominent person and has influence in the community and very rich, do you think they will speak good words about your wife or your children? If you use all that to judge your wife you are making a great mistake.

You know the truth about your husband or your wife, but choose to use bad reports and lies to judge your wife so that you have access to other women, same thing with a woman so that you can have access to another man. You will be judged for your action because you use wrong reports, which are not official. That is evil practice. You have joined the gang of evil.

Information

When you use evil reports to judge people and to condemn people and spoil things that mean you have become evil person through your own effort.

When goat feed and raise human, it becomes partial goat-child. If Satan can corner you for any reason and use evil reports from all sorts of people around you and spoil things, whom are you serving? Automatically you are agent of Satan.

Go to churches and see much confusion. There reason confusion abound in Christendom is because they believe in bad reports. Caiaphas and all the priests in the temple use bad reports to judge against Christ. Members in the church still use bad reports to turn against their preacher.

Preachers also use bad reports against their members. The Leader in the church, the senior persons use bad reports against their workers. As a result evil fire starts there. When they get rid of you, they would not believe you again. So beware of reports because evil people like reports so that they use that to damage people – the **Reporters** and the **Receivers** of **Reports.**

F: **SIGN OF A GOOD LEADER**

Every good leader starting from yourself – the leader of yourself – the higherself, a father, a mother, senior brother, senior sister, family head, member of the community, councillor, president, governor, leader of a church, pastor, reverend, Kings, Queens, Prime Minister ... name it, any post or position, if you are good, you do not deal with or work with **Reports.**

If somebody comes to report somebody to you, call the two people concerned together. Let him or her repeat what he or she said before the person being reported, if you want to be good person.

If the report is threatening your life, there is a way to handle it. Be in spirit and the spirit will tell you what to do. You cannot just jump up and carry troops to kill somebody because someone paraded that the person wants to kill you. You do not know the evil plan behind the report. People act lots of films in today's world. Also people act lots of dramas. People tell so many stories to make you understand that evil is too much in this world. With these entire things you can have the sign of a good leader. You must always take precautions regarding what you heard and the action you took. You must always bear in mind that people can gang up against someone. You must know that if you are a good person, people want to spoil the good ones around you so that bad people will be around you to make you become bad.

    If you have ten people working for you, if six of them are negative, they will try to win over the other four. The more positive ones you have around you the more successful you are. That is exactly what is happening.

Information

The sign of a good leader is not hear and judge. He knows before he judges. He is convinced – he has all amounts of convictions before judging.

A true leader does not hate one and love the other. A true leader is with **MY** Spirit of **THE FATHER GOD,** who is equality in dealing.

A leader means God.

A leader means a teacher.

A leader means FATHER GOD'S Representative.

So, if you are a leader, somebody who is to lead his children and your life – starting from you life. When you are not truthful, your life cannot be truthful. That is what happens. Check everything.

In this Kingdom of God, we do not judge anybody but we do not condone evil. What is truth is truth and that is exactly what **I** put in place in the whole universe.

As a sing of a good leader, **I** have manifested in the world as **COMPLEX CENTRE OF EXCELLENCE IN**

LEADERSHIP, with humility, with love, with patience. You see **ME** tie wrapper down and t/shirt up that means **I** use humility to live on earth with man and **I** use righteousness to live with all the people in spirit. So **I AM** THE MODEL LEADERSHIP OF LIFE. Love, patience, humility, kindness, character-wise, the way **I** talk, do you hear **ME** condemn anyone? Have you heard **ME** judge anybody?

    I leave judgement for the natural way. Don't you see that **I** love everybody? **I** operate with mannerism of correctness and equality. Do you do like that? If you do not do like that you cannot say you represent the Leader or you represent yourself.

    Therefore, the sign of a true leader is a Model of A Universal Supreme Leader of God. **I AM THE LEADER!** All those who hear **ME** know **ME** and all those who search for **ME** will see **ME.**

G: DO NOT NEED A REPORT FROM HUMAN IF YOU ARE A GOOD LEADER

Human beings will never give you a good report and a truthful human being will not like to come and report someone to you.

A principles person will never come to testify against a fellow human being. Rather the person will testify about the goodness of people because the person will take good out of the bad and drop the bad part of it.

When you eat food, this is what happens. In the human system, there is refinery industry in humans. All the water you drink and all the good things that enter into your system, **I** refine them, naturally in your system. **I** retain the good part of what you ate to form blood and water in you. Then the bad part of it you generate and discharge the waste from your bowels as faeces.

If you go back to eat your faeces and drink your urine that means you bring evil back to yourself and you will be ill. So, the blood that remained in you is refined. **I** refine it again and it became supernatural refinement.

At this stage you have red blood and water. Then **I** have the water and blood mixed again called sperm, stored in men. This sperm, which is semen, must come from the marrow of your bone. When you meet a woman that is what you pass into the woman's system to have a child. In this manner that child resembles you. That is the way **I THE FATHER GOD** operates that is, life – nature operates.

With this system, which one are you going to take? Are you going to take the system in which someone would sit down and think – 'How will **I** separate this husband and wife? They love themselves too much. How will I spoil this man that has become too popular? It is like only him or her that exists. How will I damage his or her name? Jealousy, strife and envy and arrogance cause people to do what they are not supposed to do.

Politicians and indeed almost everybody wants to be on top. Before they can be on top they have to remove the top person. You cannot be on top of a person. That position must be vacant. How will they do it? They go about spoiling the one that is there, so they can be there. This is what happens, the satanic system.

So, do not take **Report** from persons. Take the **Reports** that you know by yourself. So that you can proudly know that you know.

That is the end of Part Three of this Lecture Revelation **REPORT.**

INFORMATION

PART FOUR:
REPORTERS

A: **WHAT IS A REPORTER**

B: **WHO REPORTS WHOM**

C: **THE WORK OF SATAN IS TO REPORT**

D: **THE POSITIVE AND NEGATIVE NEWSCASTER**

E: **EVIL PEOPLE LIVE BY INFORMATION FROM MAN'S REPORT**

F: **SPIRITUAL REPORTERS**

G: **WHAT KIND OF A REPORTER ARE YOU**

Information

Those are the subtitles **for the Part Four of this Lecture Revelation – REPORTERS**

A: WHO IS A REPORTER

As **I** said earlier, **A Reporter** is somebody that goes about looking for news and reporting news Newscasters. They are agents for fetching **INFORMATION.** Is a **Reporter** servant of God or servant of evil?

You can make reports, but how many people fast and pray and practice what is good so that they can GET DIRECT INFORMATION from **THE FATHER GOD** and then report to human beings. Since everybody is not practicing love some people's mind is not good. So many people are practicing evil. So, **I** decide to deal with everyone individually.

I, THE SUPREME WORD OF THE UNIVERSE, I AM inbuilt in every individual human beings, but **I** give people different talents so that you can still link with one another in love. Sometimes what **I** give you, **I** do not give the other one. Sometimes what **I** give the other person, **I** do not give to you so, that **I** will not render anyone useless. That interweaving still means one spirit, but diversity of gifts or talents. For that reason you do not really need too much report from human beings. What you need is co-existence of love.

Nonetheless, **What Type Of A Reporter Are You**? What does a Reporter stand for?

Reporters are people that report voluntarily, or are appointed, or are chosen as agents for God or Satan to give the mind of God or to give the mind of Satan out to people. They are **INFORMATION Gatherers, Searchers** and **Reporting.** That is the meaning of **Reporters.**

Reporters are those who report words. You cannot report anything other than **WORDS**, events which consists of what you see, what you

Information

hear and what you know. Those are what you report, but not what you think. If you report what you think, you may be wrong, unless you are a positive tinker.

This **INFORMATION** you are hearing now is not from thinker or philosopher. It is **INFORMATION OF TRUTH.** If you get this **INFORMATION** as you are hearing now and it is **THE TRUTH,** truth events and the true position of things that are going on. Then it is from the MIND OF TRUTH.

If you have any reason to be positive and anything good, then give this **INFORMATION** out to other people. That is the meaning of being a **Reporter.** You must be a positive **Reporter.** So, if you are **True Reporter** from today, you will give this **INFORMATION** to people -'oh go and visit KING SOLOMON INFORMATION SPIRITUAL LIBRARY.'

Read at least minimum of seven Lectures Revelation, Find out things there, even if it means you have to purchase them, do so. Any means you can get the **INFORMATION**, get it. When you have them, then you can now know the type of Information that is there, just like what you are hearing now.

Who is a Reporter? Gossipers are indirect Reporters. Busybody people are Reporters. A preacher that speaks the mind of God is a Reporter. Newscasters in television, radio and other media format are all Reporters. Also, firms that publish books and other publications are Reporters, because without them you may not get some Information you need. Also without news that is, vital news your paper will not be popular. You go about to cause events so that you can report that event for people to buy your paper. That is what people do.

In the world today, negative news sells more than positive news. As a result more negative things continue to happen, because Satan is happy when negative news is given. Those

Information

who go about writing negative news are agents of evil – agents of Satan, you who report negative information about someone why don't you find positive information about that person instead bad news?

When people are born nobody reports that, but when people die they report. People fight they report, but when people make peace nobody talks about it.

I use this Lecture Revelation to correct the reporting of negative news in the whole world. If all television stations, all radio stations, all newspapers can ignore all evil. They should have a newspaper, a station or radio that says Negative Information Channel. Then all Negative news should be reported there. If you want to know negative news you go there.

Then all other channels should report positive news. Then you will see **ME THE FATHER GOD** will use that to promote all positive things in all areas, in the family, in the village, in the community, in the local authority, in the state and in the country, in the company, in the religious group, in all sects of human beings and in all nations of the world.

Ignore negative news and negative dreams because Satan goes about to show you dreams so that when you start shouting, oh somebody will died – o! Oh I have bad dream – o! Then from there evil will reign, try all possible ways to ignore all negatives dreams, but be prayerful to **THE FATHER GOD**.

So, all negative news, ignore them!
All negative dreams ignore them!
All negative events ignore them!

Don't even allow people to hear that husband and wife fought. That people are going to divorce or going through divorce. When you talk about those things, you want many more people to be divorced and you want people to fight more.

Give the news that people are reconciling!

Information

People are happy!
People are jubilant!
People are fine!

Let the positive news from today reign supreme on earth in your life and starting from the family.

All nations, all countries, churches and all families that deal with negative reports will sink down. The more negative report you use to take action, the more you sink down.

If, however, you deal with positive reports, improvements, then you will be going high, high, high.

If you promote **MY WORD,** which is positive **I** will promote you very high and high-high. But if you demote **MY WORD** with negative news, **I** will demote you low-low. You know what low-low is and you know what high-high means.

High-high means life upon life and promotions and good quality of life. Low-low means subjection to spiritual poverty and abject poverty in soul and finally your soul is death. Then you will be nowhere to be found.

Information

That is what **I** advice and talked about the meaning of **Reporters.**

B: WHO REPORTS WHOM

Have you ever seen positive human beings that go about reporting things? Is it only negative people that like to report things and people, 'Oh, Papa – o, that your son did this. That your husband, I saw him carrying another woman in his car. Do you trust him? I saw that your wife smiling with somebody on the road. Do you trust her?

Who reports whom? When you take that report what do you expect? You who gave that report to scatter someone's family what peace do you have in your life? There is nowhere there is fire, if it is not someone that caused that fire. Who is that person? It is Satan using those sorts of people – disintegration people to cause problems everywhere here and there. So, if you conquer this you will conquer so many problems in life.

Information

This Lecture Revelation is one of its kinds. It is a Companion of General Life, a successful life on earth. Therefore, use Everlasting Gospel and this Lecture Revelation and other **FATHER'S TALK** Lectures to help yourself. As you have access to this one, make sure you lay hands on at least seven of other Lectures and read them and then your eyes will open.

When you report somebody, indirectly you are reporting yourself. Any day you report somebody negatively, you are reporting yourself and you are damned. You are finished! Do you think **I** judge as humans?

Nonetheless, if you promote somebody, for instance, somebody did good things for you and you promote the person that is, you talk about it, then **I** will also give you the power to do good things. You also will be promoted.

Who reports whom? You take a report and judge people then, **I** will take a report and judge you. So, be careful with the type of report you give to people and the type of report you receive from people.

C: **THE WORK OF SATAN IS TO REPORT**

That is the reason **I** said that most of the **Reporters,** most, represent evil and that is Satan because the work of Satan is to report. Satan is a roam about soul in lower-self of individual human persons.

Reporters always roam about listening to people's talks and gossips. They would go to church, different gatherings – anywhere at all. Sometimes they pay money to prostitutes to go and tempt somebody so that they have bad reports about the person they target. They are tempters!

Nevertheless, **Reporters** can also report situations to bring the secret things to light so that people would know what to do about that situation.

So, it is not all reporters that are evil, but most of the Reporters work for evil. Satan is a **Reporter; Holy Spirit is also the most powerful positive Reporter.** Who reports children of God to God? It is Satan.

When you commit sin and you are **THE FATHER'S** child, Satan will come back to tell **ME** 'oh this your child has committed sin against yourself– o!' punish him or her if not I will punish them for you, But when you are fine doing good things Satan will never come to tell **ME** you are very good, that is the work of the Holy spirit of truth to report all your positives good works.

Do you know that Satan would plan temptation for you, testing you? When you fail, he will come to tell **ME** that you have failed that **I** should judge you.

Indirectly, **I AM** not **THE FATHER GOD** that judge people or make you sick when you commit sin. It is Satan himself that does that because he wants your downfall. For instance, people say you commit sins and that is the reason you are sick or that is the reason you died or that is the reasons things are bad with you.

How many evil people die on earth?

How many evil people are sick on earth?

How many evil people do evil, that Satan really torture? You see that!

When you see something happen to evil people, it is what they sow that they reap. It is not **I, THE FATHER GOD** punishing them. **I** have never condemned anybody. **I** have never judged anybody. **I** have never destroyed anything because **I** do everything. A bad child is good in his father's eyes. Everything on earth is created by **ME, THE FATHER GOD.** Why should **I** destroy them? The evil one is the one destroying things because he is not happy since he is a wanderer.

He goes about to make nations fight against nations. So they would be destroyed. Every good place that is rich he would go to instigate the other

Information

country – look, don't you know, you will not be super-world. You have to make that country to fall. If you give that country bad president, bad houses and many bad, bad things and surround them with criminals so that the wealth they have will amount to nothing. That was what they did to Nigeria.

Some years ago, Nigeria was to be in the lead in the whole world financially and other wealth because that is where **I** buried all the things to finance the whole world.

Do you know what Satan used finance to do? Between the years 1970 to early 1980s - go back and check records, a Nigerian Naira was nearly more than British pound money. Who made Naira fall? Do you think Nigeria made Naira fall? The culprits are the gangsters in the whole world.

They said, 'Oh, this poorest African country will be as powerful in wealth, in economy as their money is high. So

Information

to counter that, they bought all the Nigeria currency, Naira. They bought, bought, bought and bought the Naira and then returned all the money in one fell swoop and dumped and flooded the country with all that naira they bought, the economy fell.

Thereafter, they went about and formed gangs and tell the people to rule Nigeria. They people that rule Nigeria is human beings of certain kind and downright questionable characters. They siphoned the country's money to their accounts in the banks abroad.

You say you do not want fraud, but when somebody, a President, a Prime Minister, a Member of House of Representative brings millions upon millions of money from looting their country's treasury and come and bank in your country, you accept. Then you indirectly use that money to trade. And eventually, you kill that man so that that money is lost. Who caused that? It is evil.

Nevertheless, any country, any community, any tribe, any human being and anybody at all in anyway that did that and are involved whatsoever, their action will reverse back to them. Your evil action will boomerang on you. You will pay for it.

IN **MY** LIFE AND IN THE POWER OF THE **WORD, THE SUPREME WORD THE CREATOR OF THE UNIVERSE, HE IS THE SPIRIT** nobody commits sin and omits paying for it unless you repent and replace good in the place of evil. What you sow is what you reap – go heaven come back! And now, majority of the countries in the world know this. Britain knows, America knows, France knows. Some of the advanced spiritual and physical countries in the world know this. So, they are now trying to be good to everybody. They are establishing goodness everywhere because through that they released they would be stable, if they are now in turn build back all those places.

Information

Whereas, previously, they thought it was to go about planting evil seeds to get rid of people and countries. No! The more you suppress people, the more it boomerangs on you. You plan evil now for your children to reap tomorrow, who is your children that will reap, it is same you who will come back and reap what you plan and left behind.

All the countries that go about suppressing people and that go about fighting people and destroying people, the evil they do will find them out. The reason **I** do not want it to happen immediately is because you will get away with it.

How many Presidents that sent people to war went to war? When you are alive now you won't go to that war. But when you die and come back you join the army and go to that war by force. You must surely die in the war! Think about it! There is nothing that you do which you will not pay for it.

Information

Do you know why **I, THE FATHER GOD** came in the name of our Lord Jesus Christ to die? The reason is that when **I** was Adam, **I** fell victim to Satan and **I** came back to pay for it.

So, as **I** came and paid for that, what did **I** say? I said that whosoever that do not carry his or her own cross and come after **ME** is not worthy of **ME.** That means that every human being must carry the cross of his or her sins. You discharged waste from your bowel, who will clean you up? It is you. Not even your child can do that for you.

It is normally said – to carry the sin of the parents to the children. This is exactly what happens. The child that carried the sin of his or her papa is not that child. It is that father that came back as the child and so pay for the sins he committed. That is exactly what happens in family roots. **I** make sure you don't reincarnate elsewhere to go and enjoy, you will born where you 'shit'. Unless where people 'shit' on your plate then, **I** will remove to plant where it is good. **I AM** the CHIEF ADMINISTRATOR in Heaven and Earth.

The work of Satan therefore is report. He goes about engineering falsehood, putting up temptation for you to fall victim. Then he will come to report to **THE FATHER GOD** that this person you think is good is bad, judge the person. **I** do not have a hand in that.

Satan is the only bad one every other person is good.

D: **THE POSITIVE AND NEGATIVE NEWSCASTER**

Reporters are newscasters, which are either positive or negative. However, you should beware of the type of news you are working with, listening to and intending to take action on. That is **MY** advice in this Lecture Revelation.

This Lecture Revelation should not be lengthy again because **I** have covered all the relevant areas. How you can use it to manage your office in anyway, even if you are God. Even if you are this **WORD** that manifested as human being, this is how you should be careful. If you are not careful, then you betray your innerself by using wrong reports to judge people wrongly. You will pay for it if you do.

E: **EVIL PEOPLE LIVE BY INFORMATION FROM HUMAN REPORTS**

Evil people collect information from you because you have no Father and you have no Holy Spirit in you. You are afraid. What you then do is you pay all the people around to give you reports, so that you will not be killed. Will that one work?

Be careful, if you are free, you are free. When you have no problem, you have no problem. When you have problem, problems follow you everywhere. The problems you have are the ones you created all by yourself.

When you use your mouth and you thoughts and your hands to create problem that problem becomes your child. It will born and reborn and reborn again from you. Nonetheless, the problems that people created for you, **I** take care of those ones. Leave those ones for **ME.** The ones you created by yourself have nowhere to go because it is your own energy.

You can't blame the evil people when they live by **INFORMATION** because they are evil. A good and reasonable person will not send people to go and eavesdrop on others and report back. What will be your gain? The downfall of somebody is your gain?

A righteous person, a good human being can never be happy at the downfall of another human being. That shows the sign of wickedness and evil if you rejoice at others demise.

If you are happy that someone has fallen or that the situation of someone is bad, your own will be worse than that.

F: **SPIRITUAL REPORTERS**

I have **Spiritual Reporters** that are working in the correct way. Everybody has guardian angels and everybody has a replica of himself or herself.

I live in your heart and in your thoughts and **I AM** the one you are speaking. So, **I** know everything about everybody and every situation. That is how **I** have **Spiritual Reports.** Therefore, nobody tells what to do. This **WORD** you are hearing that is how **I** motivate it.

I AM A SPIRITUAL REPORT MYSELF. I live in every soul. **I** created organisms and living creatures and **I** live in everything that lives and thinks. Even those that have only instinct, **I** know. So nobody can report anybody to **ME**. **I** have **Spiritual Reporters** that do that.

Every human being has soul angel that **I** assign as your guardian that reports every situation to **ME.** That is how you are going to pay for what you sow.

No position that you occupy in this world can make you bribe those angels or that reporter. You can only do that physically. Nevertheless, who is bigger than the **Holy Spirit** or the **Supreme Word**?

G: WHAT KIND OF A REPORTER YOU ARE?

Are you a positive reporter or a negative reporter who go about spoiling people's home? And who goes about causing problems here and there?

Are you that type of a Reporter? Ask yourself that question and then refrain from doing so from today if you are negative reporter. Mind your own business. Resign from that type of work.

If, however, you are a positive reporter then God will elevate you. But the negative ones cause confusions. They cause disarray and lack of peace everywhere in this world. **I** will debase you and demote you low-low! That is what it is.

This is the end of Part Four of this **INFORMATION** Lecture Revelation.

INFORMATION

PART FIVE
CONCLUSION

A: THE SUPREME REPORTER IS THE HOLY SPRIT OF TRUTH

B: EVIL REPORTERS ARE THE WORKERS OF SATAN

C: I AM THE FATHER GOD, I JUDGE ACCORDING TO WHAT I HEAR AND KNOW AND SEE.

Those are the contents titles of the last part, which is **Part Five** of this **INFORMATION** Lecture Revelation, **THE CONCLUSION.**

Today, it pleases **ME, THE FATHER GOD** to give this Lecture Revelation called **INFORMATION.** This is the last Part, which is Part Five: **CONCLUSIONS.**

A: **THE SUPREME REPORTER IS THE HOLY SPIRIT OF TRUTH**

I, THE HOLY SPIRIT OF TRUTH AM THE SUPREME REPORTER. How will you know - how will you know about this **Report?**

If **I** did not give this Lecture Revelation – if **I** did not bring this Lecture, this Revelation to mankind, mankind will not know. They would still pretend that what they do is good. And so many people would still believe that getting people to go about prying on people's lives is a good thing. It is not good. You are working for evil.

The worst part in human situation is that you would sit down living your life and someone would come to give you news that breaks your heart.

The worst thing again is that something you never thought of someone accuses you of saying it or that you did that.

Information

The worst frustration you can give to someone is that someone who has been so nice to you and honest. Then you say to him that his wife has been cheating on him. She is a prostitute. She committed adultery. The reporter swears heaven and earth, even takes photographs and did all sorts of things to show as proof; all that you do is evil.

What can evil people not do in this world, unless **I THE FATHER GOD** protects you? That is the reason that the more you detach yourself from people and live more and more by yourself, the more freedom you have. When you do that they cannot get you.

Leave the spiritual aspect for **ME.** They use witch and wizard and all sorts of things to disturb you in the dream and to frighten you. That one is different. **I** have taken care of that aspect. But physically, when you do not go to drink with people, when you

Information

do not go to mingle with evil people, you are free.

If you are working, go to your work and go home after work. Do not associate with people because you do not know what people are. Human beings are covered with so many skins, some so beautiful, but inside of them they are stinking and smelling. You cannot tell. People are so bad because of the evil spirit that lives in them.

I AM THE SOLE SPIRITUAL HOLY SPIRIT OF TRUTH REPORTING THIS TRUTH AND GIVING THIS INFORMATION, EXPOSING EVIL PRACTICE IN THE WHOLE WORLD.

Don't see how people laugh with you – 'oh you are wonderful!' They are all pretending. Read the Lecture Revelation titled, **BEWARE** then you will see in that revelation about how people behave.

People pretend too much! In the church they bend down and lie down on the ground and call you all sorts of nice names. As soon as your back is turned, they mock at you.

When people say you are very nice, check yourself properly whether you are nice. If you are really nice, believe yourself. Do not believe people.

Do not believe the title they give to you, even when they give you position with a big post and title, it is because they plan what they will get from you, is not that they love you or believe who you are. Believe what **I THE FATHER GOD** give to you and the position **I** give you because **I** the Holy Spirit of Truth judge from what **I** give you and what you stand for. **I** do not judge from what you are not.

So, this is the Truth situation - the truth about **TRUTH** – the Holy Spirit of Truth. That is what **I** want everybody in the whole universe to understand.

Generations upon generations stand by the truth. Read the Lecture titled, ***THE SPIRIT OF TRUTH.***

B: **EVIL REPORTERS ARE THE WORKERS OF SATAN**

When **I** say that **Reporter Are the Workers of Satan,** it is not all reporters, but most of them as **I** said before are the workers of Satan.

What do you report? Do you report people's good character? Do you like to even write about the good things people are doing? All you go about gathering are evil news so that people would buy your paper. That means you are promoting evil.

Even in God's way, how many people – how many preachers have good news to give? Tell **ME** since you have been a preacher or a pastor, how many people speak well about your wife or your children? Since your marriage to a preacher or a pastor how many women or men speak well about your husband or wife?

Information

They tell you that business people, particularly men always go to sleep with other women. They tell you that prominent men always fornicate. Gaining access to such information spoilt your mind. Because of that you decided to go out and do your own. As a result there is no more trust.

If you love someone you should learn to trust that person. You should develop trust in the relationship. If you go about gathering information from people, you will spoil your relationship. Sometimes, when you do not know something, you do not bother, but when you come to know it becomes sickness. When you did not hear anything you were fine, but when you heard you are no longer fine.

The more you go to tell people your story, the worse your situation gets. You will no longer have peace because every negative word enters into the mind gives you wounds.

Therefore, **Gossipers, Information Gatherers** and **Reporters** beware of what you are doing, because you will reap what you sow, if you sow for good you will reap well. If you sow for bad you will reap the bad you sowed. **I** mean it.

These WORDS came from **ME THE SUPREME WORD.** It is different from the word you think. So, no energy can take away this truth. This truth remains for eternity.

If you do not want to suffer the penalty of going about spoiling people's homes, people's family, giving wrong information to people and reporting wrong thing to people, and then refrain from what you are doing. If not continue to work for Satan and Satan will pay you for your duty.

C: I AM THE FATHER GOD I JUDGE ACCORDING TO WHAT I KNOW, WHAT I HEAR AND SEE. I DO NOT WORK ACCORDING TO WHAT YOU TOLD ME

I defend **MYSELF** when it is said, 'Oh God judges according what **HE** heard from people.' Did **I** tell you that **I** judge according to what you tell **ME?** Do **I** hear anything from man? What **I** hear is spiritually because **I AM** living in your thought. **I AM** the Silent Thought in you. So, before you plan **I** first know. Before you even talk, **I** first hear and before you even do any event **I** first see it.

I AM the activator of the heart. That is how **I** judge. **I** do not take that to compare with human judging, in the form of a preacher, in the form of a human leader, in the form of government. You judge what you hear. What do you hear? And what do you know to judge? Do you know the truth about anybody? Are you living in people's heart? Even the people that are with you, who are reporting things to you; finally **I** will expose them for you to know that they are all evil.

With their evil they send away all good things from you and they render you useless because when only evil is around you, you are finished. You have no backup!

Let **ME** explain this well. Everybody that **I** send in this world to come and work for **ME, I** also give them instrument for work. The people that will be with you are going to be good. **I** will arrange to send good assistance to you. **I** cannot send you on an errand and leave you comfortless. Nonetheless, if you send them away by yourself through your actions, now what will remain with you is evil, negative, emptiness and that when trouble comes.

When **I** give you a good husband, a good wife, a good child, a good friend, a good servant, a good supporter, Satan will start to tempt them. When you see them start to misbehave you should not judge them and do not disown them. Have patience, when that evil finished their duty and they did not succeed they will leave the person for you. That is what is happening. Check it well!

Turbulence in every relationship and every event is the test of the event. When that turbulence is finished then the actual true position of that relationship is established. That is when you will see the truth Position of things. Turbulence time – the initial time will be very sweet. That is Brotherhood. The Cross will be the turbulent time – the testing time of every situation – of every relationship. That testing time is turbulence. That is when evil does his work – at the cross. When you pass and conquer that period then it is the Star. That is when you will succeed.

Your wife will be successful.

Your children will be successful with you.

Your friends will be successful with you

Your workers will be successful.

Other people with you will be successful.

Then everything is well with you. Nevertheless, when you do not conquer the cross, forget about getting to the star.

That is **MY WORD** today. And that is **INFORMATION, REPORT AND REPORTERS** Lecture Revelation.

Let **MY** peace and blessing abide with the entire world now and forever more, Amen.

THANK YOU FATHER! THANK YOU FATHER! THANK YOU FATHER!

PRAYER BY QUEEN DISEM S D ETE:

Let thanks and praises be given to **THE FATHER GOD** in the name of our Lord Jesus Christ, Amen

Let thanks and praises be given to **THE FATHER GOD** in the blood of our Lord Jesus Christ, Amen

Let thanks and praises be given to **THE FATHER GOD THE CREATOR OF THE UNIVERSE** the Supreme Information from whence the Genesis of all Information as the Supreme Word of the Universe, the Light of the world even now and forever more. Amen

Holy, Holy, Holy Father

Thank you immensely for this Christ day once again for coming by Thyself to give this lecture on INFORMATION as the Light and as Information is the servant of the WORD. We thank you Father also for revealing that human beings are the Reporters but you are the Supreme

Information, the one that knows all things. We thank you Father that you have given all thy creations particularly human beings the ability to report positive news only and to reduce and to subjugate all negativism, Father so that the light - positivism will be promoted in the entire universe for eternity, now and forever more. Amen.

Let thanks and praises be given to **THE FATHER GOD** in the name of our Lord Jesus Christ, Amen

Let thanks and praises be given to **THE FATHER GOD** in the blood of our Lord Jesus Christ, Amen

Let thanks and praises be ascribed to the Creator of the Universe, the Information of all information of truth, even now and forevermore. Amen.
THE FATHER GOD in the name of our Lord Jesus Christ, Amen

THANK YOU

Chapter Two

MY OFFICE
===
MY OFFICE IS THE SPOKEN WORD YOU SHALL GIVE ACCOUNT OF EVERY WORD YOU SPEAK

Information

FATHER'S TALK
(GOD PRESENT)

Elijah, Thirtieth Andrew FATHER Two Thousand and Eight (CO.OE.BOOH) Friday, Thirtieth May Two Thousand and Eight (30/05/2008)

In the name of Our Lord Jesus Christ, In the Blood of Our Lord Jesus Christ, Now and forever more Amen

---

MY OFFICE
===
MY OFFICE IS THE SPOKEN WORD
: **YOU SHALL GIVE ACCOUNT OF EVERY WORD YOU SPEAK**
===========

I WANT THIS PARTICULAR LECTURE REVELATION

Information

> **SENT TO EVERYBODY AS A UNIVERSAL LETTER OF INFORMATION AND INVITATION OF THIS EVERLASTING PROGRAM OF *UNIVERSAL SUPREME WORD SEASON CELEBRATION* ON EARTH**
> ============

Today! It pleases **ME, THE FATHER GOD THE CREATOR OF THE UNIVERSE,** to give this Lecture Revelation. The title is - **MY OFFICE IS THE SPOKEN WORD.**

A: **INTRODUCTION**

I always give introduction and advised that **THE FATHER'S TALK** is not the WORD of ordinary human being. It is the SUPREME INSPIRATIONAL MOTIVATED WORD from the Archives Records of **THE FATHER GOD.**

This WORD has come to stay to educate people in order to bring people from low mentality to the spiritual higher mentality to the wisdom of God and to Higher-self, the mentality to understand the ways of God. It also has the power to rearrange human's nature for positive goodness. For this reason **I** advised that when you come across any **FATHER'S TALK (GOD PRESENT)** do not read it as a novel or listen to it as news or read it as a story.

THE FATHER'S TALK is **THE FATHER GOD PRESENT** is a CASE STUDY. It is to give you inside self-understanding so that you will be elevated and have the awareness about **THE FATHER GOD THE CREATOR OF THE UNIVERSE.**

The WORD is everything and everything of **THE FATHER GOD** manifests via the WORD. So, **I** use this opportunity to advice all the readers and all the listeners as well as all the sponsors, promoters and anybody at all that has anything to do with the **WORD**. Also those who believe **THE SUPREME WORD**, those who believe that the **WORD** is everything and that the WORD should be recognized officially, and celebrated. **I** advise you to BE IN SPIRIT, be IN SPIRIT means CONCENTRATION, just a silent concentration on the SUPREME BEING so that the **WORD HIMSELF** will have a way in you.

If you have that understanding and accept to have the ***DIVINE ATTENTION*** of God then, everything will be well. Thereafter, **THE FATHER GOD** will give you the ability to understand every word in **THE FATHER'S TALK - GOD PRESENT.**

B: **THE FORMATION OF ALL DEPARTMENTS THE WORD IS MY OFFICE**

THE SPOKEN WORD IS MY OFFICE where **I** have departments and files that manifest Object Souls to bring awareness to the physical reality from ***REAL*** to ***REALSO*** and from ***REALSO*** to ***AMISO.*** That is, from

Spirit to Soul and from Soul to the Physical presence. So, **THE WORD IS MY OFFICE. The WORD** is THE TOTALITY OF OFFICE as RECORDS.

The Spoken Word now has departments and files for keeping records of everything, seen and unseen. That is the why the **WORD** cannot be forgotten.

When you speak the **WORD** it is registered. The **WORD HIMSELF** is the Bubble of Creation. As soon as it comes out from your mouth, it is registered and that is a record. That is the file.

The recording depends on which file and what type of record the **WORD** is keeping and the Studio it came out from. Is it a positive record or a negative one? Everybody speaks the **WORD** and everybody hears the **WORD** and everyone thinks with the **WORD**. Since you are the messenger and the House of the **WORD** - the servant of the **WORD**, you cannot escape the **WORD**.

Information

I want every human being to understand that there is nothing that will make you humans, to escape the **WORD**. The Supreme Program, which is ***THE UNIVERSAL SUPREME WORD SEASON CELEBRATION*** that **I** instructed HRM king Solomon ETE to establish here on earth, is to honour, appreciate and celebrate the **WORD**. **I** know people have been celebrating Christmas Day. They also celebrate the **WORD** in different ways in their churches and denominations. Some people celebrate variously according to their inspiration.

Nevertheless, **I, THE FATHER GOD THE CREATOR OF THE UNIVERSE** has now officially introduced The Ordinance of THE CELEBRATION OF THE **WORD**. This is the Ordinance that the whole universe and generations upon generations SHOULD CELEBRATE the **WORD** seasonally and earmark the celebration period to always appreciate the fact that every living soul uses the word to live. Even when you die, you still live by the word, in spirit, in soul and in the physical.

It is therefore necessary that generations upon generations should understand this that **MY OFFICE OF WORK IS THE SPOKEN WORD.** That is why everybody must respect the **WORD** and appreciate the **WORD**.

The **WORD** is the formation of all departmental duties, labour, *instincts,* understanding and wisdom and in all fields of life. These departments are managed, directed and manipulated by the **WORD**. Each of the departments is represented in human beings.

Nobody can do anything or experience any action or instructions in the way of governing or in the way of duty, in the way of records or listening or doing anything at all without via the **WORD**. Whether by your thought or word of mouth or writing to disseminate any information all over of the universe, it is by the **WORD**. So those actions and those things form **The Departments of the Spoken Word** in diverse ways. All of them are directed and managed through human beings. Therefore, all human beings must obey and undertake this wonderful universal movement of CELEBRATION and ACKNOWLEDGMENT and APPRECIATION of the **SPOKEN WORD.**

If you do not want to appreciate this instruction to honour the **SPOKEN WORD –**

What about the **WORD** that you speak?

What about the **WORD** in your mouth?

What about the **WORD** that you hear?

What about the **WORD** in your thinking?

What about everything about the **WORD**?

That is to say that you are not going to celebrate any person's **WORD**. You are to be celebrating the

WORD that you have and that is **GOD** in **YOU**.

You do not need to believe another person own God.

Believe the God in you.
Obey that ONE in you.
Respect that ONE in you.
Honour that ONE in you.
Value that ONE in you.
That is life.
That is your God.
It is your life.

That is the first point of movement of understanding.

The reason **I AM** bringing this Lecture Revelation to support the understanding, motivation and to engineer every heart about **THE SUPREME WORD SEASON CELEBRATION** is because some people have narrow minds and so are ignorant of the spiritual facts. Even if they know, they pretend they do not know, because the negative spirit covered their mind that they should not understand things and value important things.

Information

So, life is the **WORD**.

The **MOTIVATOR** of life is the **WORD**.

The **WORD** is the life of everything.

For this reason you must appreciate the **WORD**.

Make good noise about **THE UNIVERSAL SUPREME WORD**.

Show good appreciation in whatsoever positive form and manner you can.

I AM forming a Fan Club. It is **The Universal Supreme Word Season Celebration Fan Club** for the lovers of this program.

Those who breathe the air

Those who speak the **WORD**

Those who listen to the **WORD**

Those who hear the **WORD**

Those who give and take instruction from the **WORD**

Those who use the **WORD** in all endeavours and fields of activities and the generality of life, you are the members of the **Fan Club of The Spoken Word Celebration.** You are therefore, **MY OFFICE.**

Information

As **I AM** talking now you are **MY** Agent. Every human soul is **MY** Agent and is **MY** Office. You are also **MY** Celebrants.

Therefore, as **I** value the **WORD** in you, **I** value life in you; because **I AM** life and **I** have brought out this program for good life. So, throw away:

My church
My organization
I am the president
I am a governor
I am the Prime Minister
I am a black
I am a white
I am a man
I am a woman
I am an adult
I am a child

Throw away all that. They have nothing to do with this. THIS IS THE CENTRAL POINT FOR EVERY ISSUE for HUMAN BEINGS, THE SPOKEN **WORD**, THE **WORD**, LIFE, **simple!**

This is the CENTRE FOR ASSIMILATING LOVE by all human

beings. This is THE BEGINNING OF COMING BACK TO THE GARDEN OF EDEN. Where everything started is where everything goes – **THE SOURCE** and **THE DESTINATION.** If you read the Lecture Revelation titled **SOURCE** and **THE DESTINATION** you will see what **I** mean.

This is **MY OFFICE** – the formulation Department of all **WORDS**, in action, in instructions and in fulfilment. You must therefore, fulfil this instruction. Then **I, THE WORD, THE SUPREME BEING, THE CREATOR OF THE UNIVERSE** will be happy with every soul for making good noise about **THE UNIVERSAL SUPREME WORD SEASON CELEBRATION.**

If you are a teacher, teach about this program.

If you are a singer, sing about this program.

If you are a songwriter write songs about this program.

If you make music, make music about this program.

Information

If you are Model, model your ways according to this program.

If you are a president, a governor, prime minister, a King, a Queen, a woman, a man, an adult, children, spirit, soul, human – anyone and anything at all that has something and anything to do with thinking, speaking and hearing before action, you must do all that under this Program.

This program – **THE UNIVERSAL SUPREME WORD SEASON CELEBRATION** is a SUPREME AFFILIATE SYSTEM that every soul must attach to.

Every **human being** is a **marketer** of this program. Every **soul** is a **marketer** of this program. Every **spirit** and every **angel** is also a **marketer** of this universal program.

YOU MUST MARKET THIS PROGRAM TO THE WHOLE WORLD, indeed THE WHOLE UNIVERSE, but market it to your **self** and your **life** first.

You must appreciate the fact that **I** brought to your notice that everything you do via speaking, writing, hearing, listening and thinking are all directed by **ME, THE SPOKEN WORD** in you. Before you can have the idea for anything and arrange or act on anything **I, THE SPOKEN WORD IS THE DIRECTOR**.

Therefore, all marketers of anything and any situation of life, your first marketing port is to market the program for **THE SUPREME WORD OF THE UNIVERSE** for THE UNIVERSAL SEASONAL CELEBRATION OF **THE SPOKEN WORD.** If you do this promotion and partake of the **CELEBRATION** for **APPRECIATION** of the **SUPREME WORD** then you have now signed a personal voluntary evolution to improve your life now and later in every capacity. Then you would have the conscience that you should love one another. And that -

You should have mercy for another
You should have love for another
You should have the dignity of life for one another.

You should share positive things with one another.

You should practice kindness with one another

You should have all amounts of good things with one another because every human being that speaks the **WORD** and that has the **WORD** means that you are copies of one another. It means that no human being is different from one another in the sense that you are spirits, despite the colour of your skin and the language you speak. All is the **WORD PERSONIFY** in manifestation!

When you acknowledge this fact and believe in this **WORD**, nobody can harm you. You in turn should not harm anybody or think evil about anybody because when you do that you do it to yourself. This is a common knowledge for every soul to have.

That is it for 'B' –**THE OFFICE FORMATION OF OFFICES AND THE DEPARTMENTS OF THE WORD OF GOD.**

C: **MY FILE OF RECORD IS IN EVERY HUMAN BEING**

MY FILE OF RECORD IS IN EVERY HUMAN BEING because every human being thinks, speaks and hears before taking action.

Nobody can just take any action without thinking. Nobody can hear anything without a speaker. Either you speak silently in your thought or you voice out your thought.

Nobody can act without any instruction. You can personally direct the instruction in your heart by the Supreme Thought that is, the Silent Thought in you. Everything is via the **WORD**. The **WORD** is the manifestation of THE SPIRIT, **THE FATHER GOD ALMIGHTY.**

The stupidity and ignorance stage that is, the Baby Stage of Life is gone! Take note - the people that say 'there is nothing like God. 'I should not worship anything. I should not believe in anything. There is no human being on this earth who can say he or she does not believe in the **WORD**. There is no human being that can say he or she does not believe in his or her life or that they do not believe in the fact that they *think*, *hear, SEE* and *speak*.

If you do not believe what you *hear,* that does not mean you does not *hear*.

If you do not believe in your Word that you are *saying*, that does not mean you do not *speak*.

If you do not believe what you are *thinking,* that does not mean you do not *think*.

If you do not believe what you are *doing,* that does not mean you did not take *action*, and did what the instruction says.

Therefore, with that every human soul is a debtor to acknowledge, appreciate, reverence, worship, adore and adorn **HE IS THE SUPREME WORD – THE SPOKEN WORD, THE SOUL OF THE FATHER GOD THE**

Information

CREATOR OF THE UNIVERSE, THE HOLY SPIRIT OF TRUTH.

This is a Very serious. Very, very serious Very, very, very, serious Very, very, very, very serious, Very, very, very, very, very, very, very serious program! - Very, very, very, very serious instruction! This is The **POWER "*OBEYGO*" OF THE FATHER GOD ALMIGHTY.**

MY Record File is therefore, in you. When you read the Lecture Revelation titled ***OFFICE, FILE AND CABINET THAT IS, HUSBAND, WIFE AND CHILD,*** then you will see that every human soul represents the **Record** and the **File**. And the **WORD** that registers in every soul is the department in the office working for **THE FATHER GOD.**

The **WORD** is the *Christ* of **THE FATHER GOD** - the Servant of **THE FATHER GOD** – the Son of **THE FATHER GOD.**

Your truthful son is your only truthful servant. Anybody that can serve you well must be your replica.

The person must have your inspiration. The person must believe in you and must come from you direct or indirectly.

If your child cannot represent you positively that means the child came through you physically, but spiritually and in soul he or she is not your child.

This is the Truth. It is not a law. Therefore, every human being has a choice to follow or not to follow the instruction for the **CELEBRATION** and **APPRECIATION** of the **SUPREME WORD**. If however, you don't celebrate and appreciate the **WORD** then you have yourself to blame.

D: MY OFFICE BUILDING IS EVERY HUMAN BEING

I live in every human being. The indwelling self of you is the SPIRIT – the **WORD**. The SPIRIT lives in the **WORD** and the **WORD** lives in you that is, your **THOUGHT**.

Information

Then **HE** spread out **HIS** power of energy by ***thinking***, ***speaking***, ***hearing, seeing*** and ***doing***. That is the power motivated by **THE SUPREME WORD ITSELF**.

As you now know that **I** live in everybody, as you can know things, as you can ***hear*** even now and as you can ***think***, as you can ***see*** and ***speak***, as you can take directives via the **WORD**, be humble and do what you can in all positive capacities for the good and positive production of the celebration and appreciation of the **WORD**.

THE CELEBRATION IS ONCE A YEAR, WHICH IS, THE FIRST TO THE TENTH OF THE SEVENTH MONTH OF EVERY YEAR. That is, **OA to AO of OG** of EVERY YEAR. That is the correct way of counting. It is **The Supreme New Future Counting. Old counting** from **OA to AO of AO** means from The First Day of The Tenth Month to The Tenth Day of The Tenth Month. It is a TEN-DAY CELEBRATION.

Information

You can choose any day of the ten days of the celebration period to show full appreciation and acknowledgement for the **SUPREME WORD OF THE UNIVERSE**. You will of course require a witness. You would need somebody to know that you have appreciated the **WORD** and that you have accepted this Program for *THE UNIVERSAL SUPREME WORD SEASON CELEBRATION*. That is the reason you have to link-up with **Central Operation** for the whole world, which is through **King Solomon Spiritual Library.**

King Solomon Spiritual Library where this instruction comes from that the whole human race must have a UNIVERSAL SEASONAL CELEBRATION FOR THE **SUPREME WORD** is the **Universal Supreme Operational Body "WORLDWIDE UNIVERSAL SUPREME WORD CENTRE" (WWUSWC),** this office must establishing in every home, family, town, city, state, country and nation universally connected and coordinates with **HRM King Solomon David Jesse ETE (THE SUPREME WORD CITY AND KING SOLOMON SPIRITUAL LIBRARY ON EARTH).**

I AM living in every soul. So **MY** office building is every human being. That is why **I AM** working through you.

What you use the **WORD** to do.

What you are using your thought to do.

What you use your instructions to do and to give out and the benefit, therefore, all that is the meaning that **I, THE FATHER GOD THE SUPREME WORD, THE FATHER GOD, THE SPIRIT** live in you. You are **MY** product and **MY** property.

If **I** decide not to live in you again, you are in trouble. If **I** even decide to keep mute you are still in trouble. Any action **I** decided to act against you **MY** building you are in trouble.

When you cannot have sound health,

When you cannot have happiness in life,

Information

When you cannot be comfortable in life for whatsoever reason, it means you did not treat the **SUPREME WORD** well.

Since you did not treat the **SUPREME WORD** well, you do not recognize that the **SUPREME WORD** harbours the **SUPREME SPIRIT** who is **I, THE FATHER GOD** as you harbour the **WORD** who is the **SUPREME BEING** in you. So, if you do not recognize all this, you are in trouble one way or the other.

It does not matter how rich you are

It does not matter how popular you are.

It does not matter the power that you have.

It does not matter who you are, you are in trouble if you fail to recognize these **SUPREME BEINGS** that you harbour in you.

If you check your life and yourself very well, if you deny this program, automatically you deny yourself life.

If you accept this program you automatically accept for yourself the improvement of life. **I** live in every soul. Even if you do not know **ME,** but because **I AM LOVE, I** still live in you.

However, after everyone has heard about this UNIVERSAL SUPREME PROGRAM to HONOUR **THE SUPREME WORD OF THE UNIVERSE** on television, radio, through any audio – MP3, MP4, podcast, etcetera or read it in the tabloids, magazines and what have you, including hearing it from word of mouth, mails, text messages - as a matter of fact when everyone has generally gained information about this **UNIVERSAL SUPREME PROGRAM TO HONOUR THE SUPREME WORD** from any source at all then judgement is on you for none acceptance and none compliance.

Therefore, when you come across this information, give it to your child, your wife, your husband, your mother, father, sister, brother and all your other relations. Give it to your friend, your church member, your religious groups and religious organization, any club and organization and or society you belong to and even wish to enter, give this information to them.

If anybody received this information from you, you are free of that person's blood and are innocent of that person's blood for recanting.

If anybody received this information from you, but would not accept the instruction given and join the program, there in then on the judgement day of **THE FATHER GOD, THE SUPREME WORD** will defend you.

Therefore, every human being on earth should make sure they INTRODUCE THIS PROGRAM TO A MINIMUM OF SEVEN PEOPLE. Seven means the Seven Days of the Week will bear you witness. Seven stands for **MY** SEVEN SPIRITS OF CREATION.

MY SEVEN SPIRITS OF CREATION is from the first day of the week to the seventh day of the week that is, from Adam's Day to Christ's Day *(see*

the New World Counting in the Lecture Revelation - ASTROTS AND INNERSTROTS). That will bear you witness that you have accepted this program and that you have assimilated the information and that you have also sign-up and voted for **THE FATHER GOD ALMIGHTY, THE CREATOR OF THE UNIVERSE.**

Any form of worship you adopt and any form of ways you make attributes to God before now are all elementary.

This is AN OFFICIAL PROMOTIONAL ADVANCE WAY TO RECOGNIZE YOUR CREATOR. By celebrating and accepting and disseminating this information to every human being to join you for the seasonal celebration of the **SUPREME WORD** and to respect the **WORD** that is the recognition and acknowledgement of **THE SUPREME WORD**.

By doing this, you would think twice and ask yourself, why should I take instructions from my heart to do evil to someone that the **WORD** lives in him or her?

Why should I take instruction from somebody to practice wickedness?

Why should I take instructions via the **WORD** to hate somebody or even think about it?

Why should a thought occur to me to be wicked to somebody?

Why should I listen to any spirit soul or join any cult and be wicked to anybody that harbours the **WORD**? After reasoning like this you would value the **WORD** that you are a celebrant; that the **WORD** is in you. Since you know the **WORD** and you love the **WORD** you will love every human being that has the **WORD** in them as a copy of you.

The **WORD** is only one thing but has departments and offices, which are human beings like you. Therefore, it is a must that you love one another.

You should mind your business.

You should not talk ill about people.

You should not hate anybody no matter how evil that person is. Leave their evil to them for they will pay for their evil.

Information

If anybody did bad thing to you, just forgive that person. Forgiving the person does not mean he or she will not pay for their bad deeds. It means that you are free.

I can talk endlessly about this and continue to expatiate more and more about this program because **HE IS THE SUPREME WORD** IS ALL AND ALL IN EVERY CAPACITY

Therefore, **MY OFFICE** buildings are human beings, which **I** will continue to occupy to minister this program. If you refused that **I** should live in you to administer this program so that you can live well, so that things change for good in the whole world, then you are a wanted person.

The voice you are hearing is the **SUPREME WORD OF THE UNIVERSE**.

Understanding is the **WORD**.

With no understanding you abuse the **WORD**.

Acceptance is the **WORD**.

None acceptance you abuse the privilege that **I** give to you via the

Information

WORD. If you abuse the **WORD** in any way **I** can withdraw **MYSELF** from you at any moment.

When the information about this program is properly distributed through out the entire world, when there is as many as people as possible that would have heard about this program and probably pay scant attention to it that is how severe **MY** action will be, because people think about the last day judgement. People think about the action of **THE FATHER GOD**. You have not seen anything yet!

From the time you hear about this information and you ignore it then, you are a debtor to your life because anything can happen to you any moment from that time.

I will decide on how to treat you when you give deaf ears and demonstrate stubbornness about this instruction.

I AM THE SUPREME WORD, the life you are living. If you can toy with the **WORD** and use it to disobey **ME,**

I will decide for you. You are not the one to decide for **ME.**

THIS **VOICE!** THIS **ORDER!**

THE **WORD** IN YOU IS THE DECISION MAKER. **HE** IS THE MASTER.

HE IS THE LIFE IN YOU.

HE IS THE ALL AND ALL FOR YOU, no matter how big you are. You will not even exist if **I, THE WORD** do not live in you. **I AM** YOUR LIFE!

All living organisms and all living creatures are smaller than a mite, even the tiniest of ants in **MY** presence when you compare to **ME THE SPOKEN WORD,** the life in you. **I AM** THE LIFE IN YOU.

This program that you are going to be celebrating continually forever to appreciate the **SUPREME WORD** means the life in you.

CELEBRATE AND APPRECIATE THE LIFE IN YOU! That is the title –

CELEBRATE THE LIFE IN YOU.

APPRECIATE THE LIFE IN YOU.

Don't ask questions!

Information

You ask: If I donate millions of pounds or dollars or if I donate houses and if I donate in cash or kind, who is the person to manage these things?

I know that that is the sort of question people are likely to be asking. You are the one to manage these things but the actual manager is the **WORD HIMSELF.** The Instructor is the **WORD HIMSELF.**

The **WORD** manipulates and arranges the entirety of everything because the **WORD** lives in you. Therefore, you must manage things according to the instructions that **I, THE WORD** give through you.

Let it be that you give one million pounds or one pound; one million dollars or one dollar; one million naira or one naira to appreciate the **WORD**, which is the life in you. Then this money or the donation in kind or cash and whatsoever you did in your position as a form of the celebration that yielded proceeds is apportioned out for the **WORD**. You would then

Information

send what the celebration yielded to **King Solomon Spiritual Library** via the Authorised Centre or the Approved Agent or affiliate body or whosoever that is in that category. You yourself are affiliate member.

King Solomon Spiritual Library, which is the body to manage all the revenues from ***THE UNIVERSAL SUPREME WORD SEASON CELEBRATION,*** will be connected to all nations of the world and their government's authority that handles Taxes and Revenues. Every individual country of the world is inclusive.

Then as **I** instructed on the percentage sharing of the revenue amongst all countries of the world as well as to every individual citizen of the world will be carried out. Then each country's share is recorded and Certificate of Celebration given as the Celebrant.

When you are given the certificate as the Celebrant, your donation will be there for you. If at any time you have any problems of any kind, your donation becomes something you can fall back on to relief you of your problems as your spiritual account with ME THE FATHER GOD through THE UNIVERSAL CHARITY **OUCFUND**.

This is how the WORD being **THE FATHER,** being **THE SON,** being **THE MOTHER,** being the **SUPER RELATION** will solve all humans' problems.

This is the only purse that you MUST NOT use to go to war.

This is the only account that you MUST NOT use to kill people that is, to deprive any persons of their life.

This is the only account that you MUST NOT use for prostitution of any kind.

This is the only account that you MUST NOT use for promoting evil and bad news.

This is the only account that you MUST NOT use for any form of negativism.

THIS IS THE ONLY ACCOUNT THAT BELONGS TO **SUPREME POSITIVE FATHER GOD ALMIGHTY.**

Information

The account is to be used in a positive way all over the world.

Do not trust any church.

Do not trust any organization.

Do not trust you yourself.

Do not trust anybody.

TRUST **THE FATHER GOD.**

You HRM KING SOLOMON DAVID JESSE ETE must testify openly to all hearers the manner and the ways you manage and direct this affair of the Universal Celebration of the **WORD.** Anything that is directed by **THE FATHER GOD, THE SUPREME BEING** IS DIVINE AND GOOD.

Therefore, nobody will suppress your gestures to appreciate the **SUPREME WORD.** Everything will be an open field – AN OPEN PLAIN MANAGEMENT OF AFFAIRS MANAGED BY THE **WORD**. That is the instruction via the **WORD**.

The reason **I** brought out this information in this heading is that since you are **MY OFFICE** BUILDING that means you can also be **MY** accountant. You can also be **MY** keepers. You can also be everything.

Therefore, you are the one **I** will be using to manage these affairs. So, do not ask questions about 'how my donations will be managed.' The **WORD** as is the instruction will manage your donations.

You! How do you manage your life? Is it not the **WORD** that manages it for you?

Since you were in your mother's womb and she gave birth to you and up till now, who has been taking care of you? Even if it is somebody else physically that assists you for anything it is the **WORD**. For instance, your accountant that manages your finances, is it not the **WORD** that lives in him or her? Show **ME** how you can exclude the **WORD** in every affairs of life. Therefore, relax!

If there is any single truthful person in this world that exist that person will be the Manager of *THE UNIVERSAL SUPREME WORD*

SEASON CELEBRATION ACCOUNT. That is it!

E: **I AM THE WORD INBUILT IN HUMANS AS EXTERNAL TO MY INTERNAL SELF**

Do you hear that? **I AM THE WORD INBUILT IN HUMAN BEINGS AS EXTERNAL TO MY INTERNAL SELF.**

What is **MY INTERNAL SELF? MY Internal Self** is the **SPIRIT** UNHEARABLE, UNSEEN ABLE and UNTOUCHABLE. When people talk about spirit they think it is the liquid type of gas. No! THE **SPIRIT** is **unheard-able, unseen-able** and **untouchable.** But through this **UNIVERSAL SUPREME WORD**, this THOUGHT – the SUPREME THOUGHT, **I** became heard-able. **I** became seen-able and touchable.

Anything you hear it is possible to see.

Anything you see, it is possible to touch.

Therefore, **I AM** the **WORD** inbuilt in you as human beings and that is **External to MY Internal Self**, which is the SPIRIT.

So, you are a human being. You are **MY External Self. I** link through you and that is why you are **MY OFFICE.**

The reason **I** say **MY OFFICE IS THE SPOKEN WORD** is that only you human being that can speak. Indeed any human being that can *think* and that can *speak*, that can *hear, see* and take *action*, is **MY OFFICE.** That is the reason **I** appointed you in all circumstances and compulsorily so, to be the deliverer, the promoter, the newscaster and an agent of this *UNIVERSAL SUPREME WORD SEASON CELEBRATION* **Program** on earth.

If you refused to accept this instruction, if you refused this **WORD**, to help **THE FATHER GOD** and yourself to live in peace in this world, you show yourself to be negative.

Information

As you know that evil – evil words, evil thoughts, the evil spirit souls tried to take over the world. For that **I** have reviewed **MY** duty via this universal supreme program. Since you have accepted to support this program that marks you as positive individual, if you refused to accept not to work under this office and accept this instruction you prove yourself to be oxymoron. You are another Lucifer agent, another Satan agent on earth. Then the **WORD HIMSELF** will leave you and you will be eliminated.

You are not dealing with any human being. You are not dealing with any person externally. It is just internally with your conscience you are dealing with.

You are not dealing with somebody that you would say, 'oh who is the person that speaks this **WORD** let me go and fight him.' Before you can say who speak this **WORD** let me go and fight him, fight your conscience first. Fight the thought that you are thinking whether it is not the **WORD**. That is why you are disabled.

If you think negatively about this program and questioning where this SUPREME ORDER – this SUPREME **WORD** came from, immediately you wanted to think like that **I** disable you in spirit, in soul and physical.

Nonetheless, if you accept with warmness of heart and positive mind, even if you are negative previously as soon as you accept this innovation – this **GOD-DO-ORIGINAL** (**Godology Operational Idea** – this **Supreme Ideology** of **THE FATHER GOD** you become positive.

Immediately you accept with joy and gladness to be **MY** agent, since **I** the **WORD** lives in you, since **I AM** your conscience, since **I AM** your energy of life,

You use **ME** to think.
You use **ME** to talk.
You use **ME** to act.
You use **ME** for all things.
You exist because of **ME** in you.

Information

So, you are **MY External Self. I AM** your **Internal Self.** Therefore, you and **I** are one. When you believe this, immediately you become positive. And **I** forgive all the sins you committed before this time.

Since you believe this, immediately all negative plans will die natural death in your heart, you will then become new environment for **ME** to live. Therefore, you should start to give information to people. This is the only way **I** will change the whole world for positive good.

President, governor, King, Queen...name them spirit, soul and physical, nobody is too big to obey this instruction. Equally, nobody is too small to obey this instruction since you took the formation as foetus to become a human being to speak the **WORD**. You must obey this instruction from the embryo stage to foetus in your mother's womb.

This is the gateway to everything. **I AM** the way, the life, death and the

Resurrection. That is the meaning of it.

If you ignore this **WORD** and do otherwise, then put yourself in prayer and blame your soul, your life and your physical life.

F: **YOU SHALL GIVE ACCOUNT OF EVERY WORD YOU SPEAK**

I WANT THIS PARTICULAR LECTURE SENT TO EVERYBODY AS A UNIVERSAL LETTER OF INFORMATION AND INVITATION TO THIS PROGRAM OF EVERLASTING ***UNIVERSAL SUPREME WORD SEASON CELEBRATION*** ON EARTH.

From the year Two Thousand and onwards is the generation of **GOD THE FATHER, GOD, THE FATHER GOD (HOLY SPIRIT OF TRUTH) THE TRINITY GOD, THE SPIRIT, THE WORD AND MAN.** Everyday **I** fast-forward the program to see what will happen in this world.

Wait and see and you will see ***THE UNIVERSAL GREAT CHANGE!***

Information

There will be change in your life,
Change in the weather
Change in man
Change in woman
Change in all government
Change everywhere, here and there.

I use this opportunity to inform all-I-I-I-I-I-I-I the people in the whole world, at the four corners of the earth, those who worship idols, those who respect and bow down and knock their head to idols and to any moulded thing - something that cannot speak, something that has no breathe of life: anybody that worships talisman, ring, a piece of gold, silver, mud, tree, metal, iron, anything; you worship anything. You insult yourself! You give yourself the greatest insult.

For **ME** to live in you as **THE SUPREME WORD**, the SPIRIT of **THE FATHER GOD,** a portion of **ME** lives in you and you carry **ME, THE FATHER GOD** to go bend down for a small metal **I AM** annoyed with you! Nevertheless, **I** will not take action yet until you read, hear or have access in any form to this information – until you get this message!

MY SOUL! Which is **THE SUPREME WORD** will not be happy with anybody that use **ME, THE WORD, THE SPIRIT** in you, the most precious thing – the costliest thing is life!

Nothing is greater than life on this earth! The **WORD**, the Motivator of Life – the Light of **GOD** in you! With big of **MY SUPREME SPIRIT** in you, you go to bend down for a wood! You go to kneel down for a metal, a carved image! You go to bend down to a mould – a moulded thing - something that cannot talk!

A talking phenomenon to go bend down for a silent nonentity!

You are a *mooh-mooh!*

You are *idiotikot!*

You are a very stupid and low soul in nature!

You are so cowardly!

You are so ***idiotic!***

Information

If you don't know, you should know today!

You! Look at your face to think you are a President. You are a Governor. You are a Prime Minister. You are a King. You are a Queen. You are a woman. You are a man. You are a human being. Yet you went and believed in a ring that somebody gave to you! You are a second-hand human being! Stupid of you ***idiotikot***!

Somebody else said,' take this ring, it will help you and you believe it. How can that small metal help you a grown up person like you, you suppose to be God image and likeness, it is not **MY WORD** which, that person speak? That instruction they give to you is the one that acted and not that metal! And you are so stupid to believe it, instead of believing **ME** in you, **THE FATHER GOD**!

This is the program that has liberated the whole human being! Every human being, no matter how small you are, believes **ME** in you! That is it!

Do not allow any human being in this world to tell you, 'come to me I will do this for you, I will do that for you.' You listen because you do not know who live in you! If only you would believe this and appreciate and support and are happy, then talk to **ME** in you! If **I** don't do it, know that **I** don't do it! That does not mean **I AM** deaf or **I** do not hear you.

The person that you go to and they give you instructions what do they use to give the instructions? Is it not the SPOKEN WORD? Is it language issue that is the case? It is the SPOKEN WORD in different languages. Speak to **ME** in your own language **I** will hear you!

This is the time of God! This is the only time the whole world shall know that **I, THE FATHER GOD, THE SUPREME WORD, THE HOLY SPIRIT OF TRUTH** has come to declare the truth and the DIVINE WAY OF WORSHIP. Go and read the

Lecture Revelation titled - **THE SUPREME BELIEVE.** That is the reason that if anybody says to you do not read **King Solomon Spiritual Library FATHER'S TALK GOD PRESENT** know that that person is evil and he or she wants to destroy your soul! That is the Satan that said he would not go alone to hell. But if anybody encourages you and gives you this message to read **THE FATHER'S TALK** in **King Solomon Spiritual Library,** then the person are helping your soul. Anybody that is positive will not deprive you of a positive channel.

If you are in the media of any form – Radio Presenter, TV Presenter, News Broadcaster, Journalist, Editor of the Tabloids...name them and you refused to publicize **King Solomon Spiritual Library,** *THE UNIVERSAL SUPREME WORD SEASON CELEBRATION,* **FATHER'S TALK (GOD PRESENT)** then you are a debtor to your life, which is **MYSELF** in you, the **WORD** in you. And if you are against your life, you are against yourself. Any day yourself is against you, you are arrested by your own self. If you arrested yourself, who will plead for you?

Do you know why people do not get forgiveness?

Do you know why people do not get their problems solved? Any day you are against your life and your life is against you that mean you are finished because that is your God, the greatest thing and the greatest phenomenon.

Anything that can help you is your own self that pleads against other selves. Other selves could be enemies and so if your life becomes your enemy then, you are finished in spirit, in soul and in the physical. That is the secret **I AM** revealing today!

This Lecture Revelation is very, very important!

This information is very, very important!

As a matter of fact, it is so important and that is why **I AM** instructing everybody that THIS IS A GATEWAY TO NEW LIFE.

This is the gateway to liberty.

This is the gateway to problem solving.

This is the gateway to the remedy of everything!

This is the universal problem solver.

Everything good! This is the gateway!

God's time is the best and **MY** season is good. **I** have been keeping quiet and observing things. **I** have the experimental stages of life in all the planets of manifest and for all generations till now. **I** have now come via this information.

Do not ask where God is. God is where you find yourself. Wherever you find yourself and you can **think**, you can **speak** and you can **see** and **hear** that is where God is. God is **everywhere**, **here** and **there**. **HE** is a phenomenon that the more you look, the less you see.

You are closer to the **WORD**. Since you are closer to the **WORD**, the **WORD** is closer to you than your tongue is to your teeth. It is right inside of you.

That is why you are a *celebrant* and **MY OFFICE**.

That is why you are the *accountant* to this program.

That is why you are the *promoter* of this program.

That is why you are **Fan Club Member** of the **WORD**.

That is why **I** order you to carry out this *information* to introduce this program – **THE UNIVERSAL SUPREME WORD SEASON CELEBRATION** to at least seven human beings. Then you will be free in the first stage of it.

G: **THE WORD IN YOUR HEART IS SUPREME JUDGE**

Do not think that you can go to hold somebody responsible for this

Information

thing. 'Oh this **WORD** is too powerful! Who speak this **WORD**?'

You want to know who speak this **WORD. THE WORD SPEAKS THE WORD!** You remember when our Lord Jesus THE CHRIST said, 'Before Abraham I was.' The Jews, because they had baby spirit, which is lack of understanding, they went to Jesus Christ and killed HIM, thinking that it ended there. Since they did that killing, did the **WORD** die?

In fact the killing of our Lord Jesus Christ promoted the **WORD** more than anything else. That is the glory of **THE FATHER GOD**.

If people say, 'That King Solomon David Jesse ETE, if I can lay hands on him,' you are joking! You cannot lay hands on Him! You can only lay hands on yourself of this **WORD** you are hearing now. You cannot lay hands on Him; you can only lay hands on your conscience and your thought.

Before you can even begin to entertain the thought to lay your hands on HRM King Solomon David

Information

Jesse ETE, you have to count all the sands on this earth and count all the hairs on your head before you can even begin to think evil about where this **WORD** came from.

If you cannot count them then, you are an everlasting debtor to think evil about HRM King Solomon ETE or about any human being at all for that matter. By thinking evil of anybody that breathes, that has the **WORD** in them that **I** live in that person, whoever or whatever that person is, and you think evil or any manner of wickedness about that person and the **WORD** lives in the person, you are everlasting debtor and a condemn soul. That is why you see the judgement of God is right in your conscience.

Before anybody can think on how to kill another human being it shows that that person is an animal. That instinct is of animal.

As **I** revealed that this world, **THE SUPREME FUTURE**, it is the Human-Gods that will be in control. So far this world has been controlled by human-animals, the aliens from different planets that have no sympathy. They are not created in the image and likeness of God. They existed as wild creations before **I** came and planted **MYSELF** on earth through the creation of Adam and Eve.

When **I** planted **MYSELF,** the wild spirit came and infused her instinct into Eve and Eve infused it into Adam via the Serpent. As a result of that evil instinct of human animal got into him that wild attitude of killing, telling lies, do all sorts of evils. Evil thoughts and good thoughts became the living partners in the human self. Now! **I** will use this program to eradicate that.

The problem started in Heaven. In Heaven **I** ordered that the **SPOKEN WORD** should be earmarked for honour and glory to **ME**, because everything is in spirit. If nothing manifests physically, it has no meaning. Everybody and everything is one thing in spirit, but if that thing does not come to pass physically it has no meaning to life here.

You can be rich. You can be very important or anything remarkable in the dream, but if you cannot be any of those things here, it has no meaning. That is why all the manipulations of witchcraft and evil people in the dream have no meaning. Do not worry yourself when you have dreams of witchcraft of VAMPIRE Cain, because it has no meaning. **Cast and Ban it!** Ignore it! Superimpose it with the Supreme Thought, the positive thought. Their actions have no meaning because they cannot by-pass **ME** the POSITIVE SELF to materialize their evil plans physically here if you believe in **ME THE FATHER GOD ALMIGHTY**. So, you will not die. Even if you saw that they cooked and ate you, ignore it because you are the **WORD**. If you believe this instruction, believe **ME THE FATHER GOD, THE SUPREME WORD OF UNIVERSE,** and understand and accept this program,

I will make you one with the Soul of the **WORD**.

Since **I AM** in you and you in **ME,** you and **I** have become one in the **WORD**. They can cook you and eat you it does not mean anything because **I** have so many souls, which are animals, fishes, birds and humans. **I** also have the Supreme Soul, which is the **WORD**, the Air. So, if **I** become the Supreme Soul for you as **WORD THE CHRIST** they cannot kill any soul in you, **I** will not let them. Nonetheless, you will still be alive because what actually gives you light both physically and spiritually is the **WORD**. It is **THE SUPREME SPIRIT AIR**.

When the evil people hear this information, they will not be happy. But it has no meaning, because it is always the truth. When you know the truth, the truth shall set you free. This is the truth that will set you free in the whole world!

All evil tendencies, all Satanic operations are melted away from the time you accept this program. And everybody is going to be free under this earth! Therefore, you value life! Read the Lecture Revelation called **VALUE –Chapter One & Two.** Then you value life, value the **SPOKEN WORD**. You will value yourself and then you will have liberty. You are free!

This is an indirect judgement that **I AM** giving to the entire universe. There is no other judgement than this. **YOUR CONSCIENCE IS YOUR JUDGE.**

If you *think* well, you *speak* well and you *hear* well and *do* well then well, well, well and good, good, good will follow you.

If however, you *think* negatively, you *think* evil, if you *speak* negative, you *speak* evil and if you *hear* negative, you *hear* evil and at the end you *practice* evil then, evil, evil and evil will follow you. That is how you are judged. All will start from your contents that is, in your own conscience, in your heart. That is what **I AM** declaring today. ***OBEYGO!*** Of **THE FATHER GOD ALMIGHTY**

CONCLUSION A: **USE ME ARIGHT**

From today, as you have accessed to this information, use the **WORD** – the Thought in you – the **WORD** via the THOUGHT and the one you are hearing very, very well. **Use ME Aright.** That is **ME** the **WORD**. Do not look for God elsewhere. Look for **HIM** in your own contents.

When anyone dies, the **WORD** comes back to where it came from. Your soul will then face the music of what you have done on earth. If you respect the **WORD** and *think* well, *speak* well, *hear* well and *do* well then, all become well. You will then become a manifestation of the Supreme Servant of God to offer help. Then you are happy in your soul. Therefore, use this information well.

As you are **MY OFFICE ON EARTH, MY** Representatives that **I** said 'Let us create man, humankind in our own image and likeness.' What is man? He is the building where **I, THE SUPREME WORD** live.

I ignored this for many, many generations because **I** did not have access back to human. So, after **I** came and died and shed the blood, now **I** have come back as the Supreme Holy Spirit, the last Personified **WORD**. And **MY** SPIRIT lavishly covers the space, everywhere, here and there.

I hear you.
I see you.
I touch you.
I feel you.
I live in you, in your conscience.

So, use it well. Without which **I** will take action against you, in the inside of you.

CONCLUSION B:
CELEBRATE THE POWER OF LIFE ENERGY WHICH IS THE WORD IN YOU

That is all what you are celebrating about the program for **THE UNIVERSAL SUPREME WORD SEASON CELEBRATION**. Celebrate **ME** in you The Power of Life, The Life Itself, which is the energy in you that is what you are celebrating.

Paying electricity bill is not that important.

Paying gas bill is not that important.

Paying any tax is not all that important.

Paying all those bills are not as important as celebrating the **WORD SEASON**, the life in you, because if you are not alive how are you going to consume electricity to pay the bill.

If you are not alive how are you going to pay gas bill?

If you are not alive how are you going to pay tax and be a good citizen to the government?

So, this **UNIVERSAL SUPREME WORD SEASON CELEBRATION,** the government of any land should take it very seriously. As a matter of fact the percentage **I** instructed to be given to the government of any land is enough for any government to add and use to run the country.

The government of any land represents God. Every human soul should respect the government of any land. And the government should not give order that is negative.

Government should not go to war.

Government should not go to kill people.

Government should not do anything negative.

Government means God.

Government is a common purse for every human citizen – every human being on earth. The whole world is one God, one CREATOR, ONE SUPREME **WORD** and ONE

GOVERNMENT OF **LOVE UNITY AND PEACE**

If you cut a portion of the world to rule with wickedness, this **WORD** will judge you. The **WORD** will judge the Judge of every Judge of the land.

Every government, every President, every King, every Queen, every Prime Minister, Head of anywhere and anything, a man, woman, a child – every living creature, living organism, every living human being, THE SUPREME **WORD** – in your conscience will judge you. This is the truth judgement that you hear about.

Therefore, the **WORD** you are hearing now wants you to cooperate with **HIM** in your heart in the contents of positivism to change this world, so that every **WORD** that manifests here on this earth plane should not face problems again, for it is **ME** the **WORD** that you are putting through suffering.

When you beat another human life, you are beating **ME!**

When you slap another human life you are slapping **ME!**

When you shoot another human life with gun, you are shooting **ME!**

What do you think you are doing? It is self, fighting against self. That is because you are very narrow in understanding. You are a baby spirit! Satan! Elementary spirit means Satan. It means mistake.

All the time you hate another human life or another human being, you are doing that to yourself. You don't know that the hatred you harbour for another person is yourself you hate. It is just like you standing in front of a mirror beholding your image. Then you hit that mirror and broke it!

When you break the mirror, it is not the mirror that you actually broke. You fought against your picture that appeared in the mirror! You see!

When eventually you don't find yourself again in the mirror, you don't know how you look like. You look very ugly when you hate another life! You are a dead soul.

This life is unique! Do you know that one bubble of life is the life of everybody on earth? One Adam and Eve is every man and woman on earth. Whether you call yourself Muslim, whether you call yourself Christian, whether you call yourself Judaism, whether you call yourself Buddhist or Sikh, whether you call yourself the first man or the last man, it does not matter. It means one life, FATHER GOD THE UNIVERSAL SUPREME WORD IN ADAM.

Respect life! Value life! Value the **WORD**! Love is the *remedy*! Love one another. That is, another life should love another life and treat another life with respect, with dignity! That is the meaning of God. **GOD MEANS ONE SINGULAR THAT BECAME PLURAL. I** have spoken enough about this. Now! **I** need action! Then you shall be blessed.

Blessed are those who listened to this instruction and have sympathy, love, humility, mercy, kindness, equality, peace and truth with one another. All is now well!

The negative self of your life said that there should not be unity on earth. There should not be equality on earth, rebuke that self in you and ban it outright for life. Those who are very rich are annoyed when they hear that everybody should be just as rich.

Everybody should be the same. Tell **ME,** you who think that you are better than another person, what type of life are in you? Is it not the same air you are all breathing?

Is it not the same life you are all living?

Is it not the same womb of a woman, a copy of Eve that bore you?

The reason you are going to answer query from **ME** – from THE SUPREME **WORD** is because you suppressed other lives. Then in turn those lives would fight against you in spirit and in soul.

Love everybody!

Love the Brotherhood!

Fear God!
That is, respect this **WORD**!
Honour this **WORD**!

That is the salvation for you. The judgement for you is when you give deaf ears and argue about this instruction. That becomes automatically judgment. It becomes voluntary judgement you have taken for yourself. It would not connect to anybody.

CONCLUSION C:
ALL IS WELL WITH YOU IF YOU BELIEVE THIS MESSAGE

This is the blessing part of it. You are all celebrants of **THE UNIVERSAL SUPREME WORD SEASON CELEBRATION.** The celebration power of life energy, which is the **WORD** in you, motivated you to accept this program and acknowledge it and get connected and start to believe that you should love one another. You should be peaceful with one another; you should do something to help another human being. Helping another human being is helping your life. When this happens the whole world shall be in peace. You can travel from here, the Western World to anywhere in Africa without Visa and without passport, without barriers and boundaries and vice versa. **I** did not create boundaries and barriers. Does it mean you will no longer return to the Garden of Eden?

It was after Adam committed the sin that **I** sent Adam away from the Garden of Eden and created a boundary. So the whole world is still in that suffering because you have not entered back into the Garden of Eden by loving one another. Nevertheless, through these directives, **I** give everybody the certificate to re-enter into the Garden of Eden where everybody lives amicably with peace, unity and love.

No human-animal should fight. Those who fight and those who kill are animals, fish and birds. They are not true human beings.

A true human being has sympathy of life. There are people on this earth that can't even lay hands on anybody to beat them much more killing them or committing any wicked act in any manner to a follow human being.

I also know that many people that do wicked things are not their doing per se. It is not them that do those things. It is the evil spirit that would enter into them to commit those wicked acts sometimes because of money.

The creation of money was to make life easy for co-existence. The creation of money was to help the Mother God, the Spirit of Mundane, to distribute the Mundane Wealth equally to everybody. But Satan uses it now to kill people, to suffer people, to do all sorts of bad things. Nevertheless, now **I** have come to take over. Through you in **ME** and **ME** in you sign up for the truth today. Sign up for this program then, **I** will be with you and you will be with **ME** to eliminate evil on earth!

If you do not sign up for this program to eliminate evil, that means you are evil, then **I THE SUPREME SPIRIT OF GOD** who is **THE SUPREME WORD** will eliminated you.

Some people will sleep and would not wake up again because they do not like this program. You do not need to fight anybody for **ME.** It is a very simple thing. If you remove the air from a football, if you kicked the ball it would not fly in the air.

If you deflate the tyre of a car, the car would not move smoothly when driven. If you removed the engine from a plane, the plane would not fly when propelled to do so. So, it is a very simple thing.

I AM the driver.

I AM the pilot inside you.

So, when you refuse to treat **ME** well, to treat another human being well, to take this instruction, **I** know what **I** will do in you.

Whatsoever position you think you occupy, whatsoever secret society, wherever you keep yourself and you think you know, whether you are a soul, whether you are a spirit or human being, whether you are an angel **I** know where you are and what to do with you.

Then those who follow this and respect and are obedient are blessed. Obedience is the first order in Heaven and on Earth. If you obeyed like every other angel apart from Lucifer who disobeyed then by accepting and believing this message, you are blessed.

Let **my** peace and blessing abide with you and the entire world and all positive children of god, now and forever more. Amen

In the name of Our Lord Jesus Christ, In the Blood of Our Lord Jesus Christ, Now and forever more Amen

THANK YOU FATHER!

Information

Prayer by HRM Queen DISEM:

Let thanks and praises be given to the Creator of the universe in the name of our Lord Jesus Christ Amen

Let thanks and praises be given to the creator of all things in the blood of our Lord Jesus Christ, Amen

Let thanks and praises be given to the Supreme Spirit that manifested the WORD that, manifested all creations who have come, we should worship and acknowledge **HIM** in the celebration of the word season even now and forever, Amen.

Holy! Holy! Holy **FATHER.** Thank you immensely for this day for the lecture you have given, the revelation you have given to give us the wisdom and understanding to know that without the WORD nothing will exist. And you the Supreme Spirit that manifest the WORD in us that lives in us. We acknowledge and appreciate the Word as lives. By so doing we appreciate ourselves and by so doing we appreciate all creations and by so doing we acknowledge and worship you the creator of all of us so that there would be peace and harmony and all will be well in the entire universe and for all creation to benefit even now and forever more. Amen!

Let thanks and praises be given to the Supreme word in the name of our Lord Jesus Christ, Amen.

Let thanks and praises be give n to the Supreme creator through the blood of our Lord Jesus Christ. Amen

Let thanks and praises be given to the A to Z, the Existence, the WORD the manifested all things, seen and unseen, touch-able and untouchable - everything under this creation, everything under this universe, even now and forever more, Amen!

THANK YOU FATHER

Information

Chapter Three

THE INSPIRATIONAL WRITER

Information

KING SOLOMON SPIRITUAL LIBRARY

THE GOD ENCYCLOPAEDIA WORD OF INFINITY

INSPIRATIONAL WRITERS AND READERS OF THE FATHER'S TALK (GOD PRESENT) KING SOLOMON SPIRITUAL LIBRARY

In the name of our Lord Jesus Christ In the blood of our Lord Jesus Christ Now and forever more, Amen

(A) REFERENCING THE FATHER'S TALK (GOD PRESENT) IN KING SOLOMON SPIRITUAL LIBRARY

I know some people will inspire when you visit King Solomon Spiritual Library website or bookshop, and have access to any of **THE FATHER'S TALK (GOD PRESENT)** information through books, electronics, audio and otherwise and are inspired to write or produce any information through the knowledge that you have gained, you must not fail to reference **THE FATHER'S TALK (GOD PRESENT)** in **King Solomon Spiritual Library** as the such of your inspirations.

(B) THE WORD OF TRUTH AND THE HOLY SPIRIT PRINCIPLES

Since **THE FATHER'S TALK (GOD PRESENT)** is the direct information from **THE FATHER GOD ALMIGHTY HIMSELF,** all positive children of God can be, and will be inspired with this **WORD** because the Word of **THE FATHER GOD, THE CREATOR OF THE UNIVERSE** is a Spiritual Case Study for all souls to improve to have self awareness and a Higherself Consciousness.

When you are inspired and you want to write, make sure that your ideas, principles and concepts base on the Holy Spirit of Truth without changing the ordinance of the **FATHER'S TALK (GOD PRESENT).**

(C) THERE SHALL BE CONSEQUENCES THAT WOULD FOLLOW THOSE WHO USE THE MEANING, THE CONCEPTS AND THE PRINCIPLES OF THE FATHER'S TALK (GOD PRESENT) FOR THE PURPOSES OF MISLEADING

Consequences shall follow those who use the meaning, the concepts and the principles of **THE FATHER'S TALK (GOD PRESENT)** for the purposes of misleading in any manner.

Any Human-God, human-animal, human-bird or human-fish who has access to **THE FATHER'S TALK (GOD PRESENT)** through any means, be it via books, electronics, audio and otherwise should know that those words are not the words of human beings. The words are transcribed, proofread and accepted by **THE**

Information

FATHER GOD as it comes from the **SUPREME STUDIO OF THE ALMIGHTY FATHER GOD HIMSELF,** via **King Solomon Spiritual Library.** When the signal of the information alerts HRM King Solomon David Jesse Etteh from **THE FATHER** through the **COMPREHENSIVE MEMORY OF GOD** in him, at anytime in the day or at night and anywhere, whether on the road or any public place, he will take note of the title of the Revelation Lectures. Sometimes if the location is conducive, lectures can take place immediately. If the location is not conducive, **THE FATHER** fixes the time for the full lecture to take place. Most of the time, some of the lectures take about a week, a month or six months and so on, to deliver when **THE FATHER** brings it back from **HIS SUPREME MEMORY** to HRM King Solomon ETE.

Take note that the information of **THE FATHER'S TALK (GOD PRESENT)** is not preaching, or the giving of sermons or shared discussion. **THE FATHER** calls it "***LECTURE REVELATION***", which is a Spiritual Case Study for mankind to improve and have the Higherself Consciousness about himself or herself and their creator. For that reason, every human being that comes across any of this information of the **FATHER'S TALK (GOD PRESENT)** should treat it with utmost and absolute respect and reverence at all times.

HRM King Solomon David Jesse Etteh is not responsible for **THE FATHER'S TALK (GOD PRESENT)** but **GOD HIMSELF. THE ALMIGHTY FATHER** only uses him as a way through, just like a loud speaker from the radio or television receiver.

For this reason, HRM King Solomon David Jesse ETE will not be held responsible by anyone who does not understand the contents, the concepts and the principles of **THE FATHER'S**

Information

TALK (GOD PRESENT) information in King Solomon Spiritual Library. He will not answer any questions or queries from spirit to soul and the physical truth in connection to the above from the lower mind individuals, persons or groups. However, if you are positive and you have love, you are humble, have patience and are peaceful and you want to know and understand more of any part of **THE FATHER'S TALK (GOD PRESENT); 'You should use fasting and prayer'** and or if anyone has any questions in good faith, he or she is free to write to HRM King Solomon and **THE FATHER** in him will respond. He will not, and there is no response to any questions, queries and anything negative with the craftiness of the evil minds of humankind.

That is why you should first read

THE FATHER GOD with **HIS SUPREME HOLY SPIRIT OF TRUTH** will bless all those who read and accept this information with good faith through the name and blood of our Lord Jesus Christ. Amen.

In the name of our Lord Jesus Christ In the blood of our Lord Jesus Christ Now and forever more, Amen

"THEUNISAL-SUREME SEACELION"
The Universal Supreme Season Celebration

========

"THEUNI-SUREME WORA THECRO-THEUNISE"
The Universal Supreme Word Almighty
The Creator Of The Universe

================

WWW.COME4WORD.COM

THE OFFICIAL SITE FOR

==============

EVERLASTING UNIVERSAL ALL WORD

SEASON APPRECIATION CEREMONIAL PROGRAM

==========

THE UNIVERSAL SUPREME

ALL WORD

SEASON

Information

CELEBRATION
(GOD PRESENT)
SOMETHING MORE THAN
GOLD
IN THE HEART OF ALL MEN IS THE
WORD

====================
THE WORD IS THE MAKER, THE SOLE ADMINISTRATOR AND THE CREATOR OF THE UNIVERSE.
THEREFORE, ALL MANKIND ON EARTH MUST APPRECIATE THE WORD IN ALL CAPACITIES FOREVER
============

FROM EVERY
OA OF AO TO AO OF AO
(1st OCTOBER TO 10th OCTOBER.)
YEARLY IS
THE UNIVERSAL SUPREME

ALL WORD SEASON

CELEBRATION TO APPRECIATE
THE FATHER GOD ALMIGHTY

Information

WORDWORDWWORDWORDWORDWORD

CELEBRATION!
CELEBRATION!!
CELEBRATION!!!

THE
UNIVERSAL
SUPREME
WORD
CELEBRATION
OF ALL TIME

Information

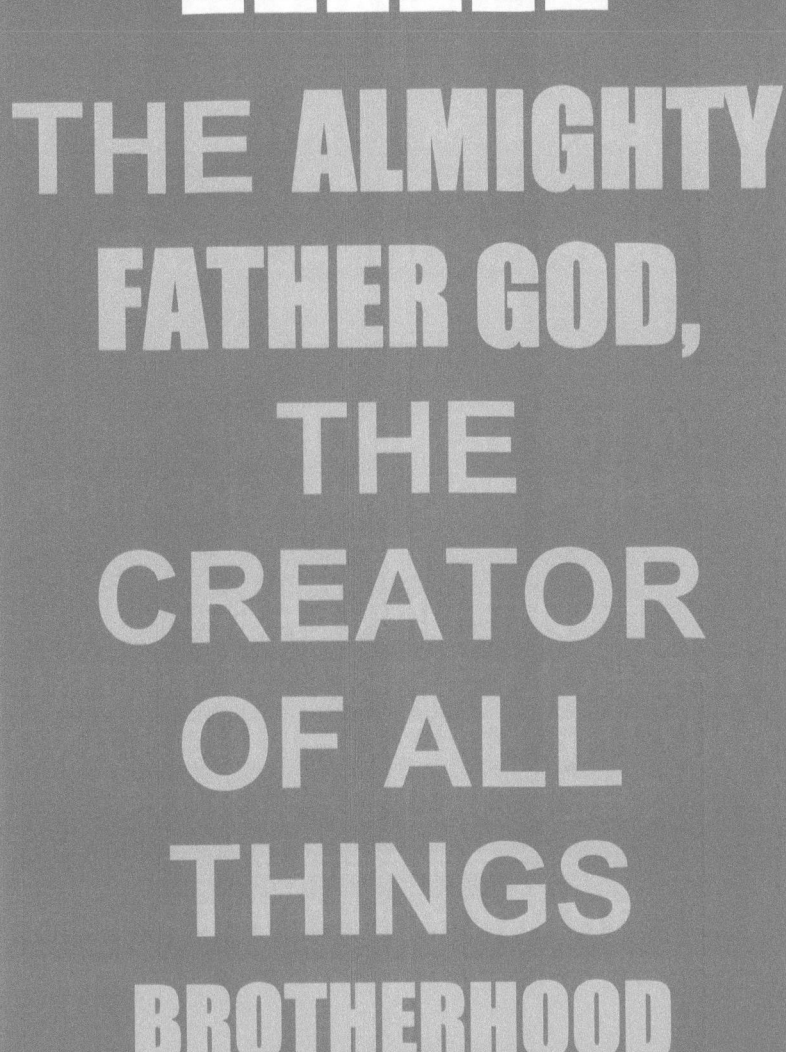

KING SOLOMON SPIRITUAL LIBRARY

======

HRM KING SOLOMON DAVID JESSE ETE
INSPIRATIONAL HEAD

IN THE HONOUR OF THE
FATHER GOD THE CREATOR
OF
THE UNIVERSE
THE HOLY SPIRIT OF TRUTH
AND THE KING OF KINGS AND
THE LORD OF LORDS

==========

THANK YOU FATHER

KING SOLOMON SPIRITUAL LIBRARY

Information

THE GOD ENCYCLOPAEDIA WORD OF INFINITY

King Solomon Spiritual Library,
God Universal Information Centre
Father's Talk (God Present)

WITH LOVE

Covered: **This BOOK,** e-book, software or software's, books, website, video, audio, idea or ideas, formula or formulas, manual or instruction manual.

... Hereby gives you a non-exclusive license to use the ... (THIS BOOK).

Information

Some of the word here is coded with the (WORD OF SUPER HOLY AND INTELLIGENCE FATHER GOD ALMIGHTY)

Title, ownership rights, and intellectual property rights in and to the Website, Books, E-book, Audios and Videos, Shops and Store – e-Stores, Fundraisings, Celebrations and the supreme word seasons Celebration formulas and arrangement, Positive Inspiration, Holy (Fata), FATHER GOD ALMIGHTY POSSESSING SPIRIT in thought, in words and in did, thinking well, speaking well, hearing well and doing well shall remain in me and in ... The BOOK is protected by international copyright.

FATHER'S TALK (GOD PRESENT)
The message in The Father's Talk (GOD PRESENT) does not challenge any authority either individuals, groups or governments of any land or even

any belief of any form. It is rather challenging the truth that is hidden from mankind. Therefore, any spirit, soul or physical human being who decides to challenge this truth shall have himself or herself to blame.

Key A

Any individual that reads any of The Father's Talk (GOD PRESENT) with faith; love and acceptance will experience immediate positive change in his or her life from spirit, soul to physical. If he or she accepts the message then he or she will be free from any evil.

Key B: **PEACE AND LOVE**

If you do not believe the contents of any of The Father's Talk (GOD PRESENT) it is possible through The Father's divine love and peace simply hands over your copy to a friend or somebody else that would like to keep a copy, or signing out from any of the website that connected to The Father's Talk (GOD PRESENT) KING SOLOMON SPIRITUAL e-LIBRARY without any evil and negative comments and you are blessed and free.

========

FROM THE DESK OF INSPIRATIONAL HEAD

Fees, Prices and Donations; There is no refund on fees, price or donations since your fees price or donations are using as a charity contribution to do administration work of THE SUPREME WORD, So please kindly read this first before you decide to involves yourself in any of the under mention of HRM King Solomon David Jesse ETE universal Inspirational Businesses of (GOD PRESENT) in cash, kinds and otherwise.

I CAME FROM THE FATHER GOD, WITH THE FATHER GOD, AND BY THE FATHER GOD TO ESTABLISH THE FOLLOWING:

Therefore, all distributors and contributors of The Father's Talk (GOD PRESENT), The Spiritual Advice, Healing and Counselling on General Live (The Universal Supreme Spiritual General Hospital), New Songs and Psalms of King David and Solomon, The Word of **GOD** Processing City in Ikot Okwo or e-City online, The Trinity Celebration, "**OUC FUND**", The Universal Bank Account For All Creations, "**ERUFA**" ETE Royal Universal Family, "**THEUNISAL-SUREME SEACELION**" The Universal Supreme Word Season Celebration To Appreciates THE FATHER GOD ALMIGHTY "**THEUNI-SUREME WORA THECRO-THEUNISE**" The **Universal Supreme Word Almighty, THE CREATOR OF THE UNIVERSE** should attach this information to all readers, website visitors, distributors, affiliates person/group, celebrant and celebrations centres, supporters and promoters, members, workers and voluntary workers, Ete royal universal palace committee, governments and many other centres as an agreement. Please kindly know that I am not answering to any physical human except **PEACE, UNITY AND LOVE.**

"THEUNISAL-SUREME WORA THECRO-THEUNISE".

I AM IN THE STAGE OF SUPER HOLY AND INTELLIGENCE FATHER GOD POSITIVE MADNESS OF THE HOLY SPIRIT OF TRUTH, ENYEN ODUDU ODUDU ODUDU ABASI MI OOO ZIM ZIM ZIM ASSASU, POSITIVE POSITIVE POSITIVE. UKEMEKE AKA IDIOK UNAM.
Let the peace and blessing of the Holy Father abide with everybody who corporate with this divine Father's Talk (GOD PRESENT

THANK YOU FATHER

BY
THE HOLY SPIRIT OF THE FATHER GOD
THROUGH HIS SERVANT

Senior Christ Servant
HRM King Solomon David Jesse ETE
Brotherhood of the
Cross and STAR
Eteroyal Universal family
Ikot Okwo The Great City of Refuge, Ete Community
Ikot Abasi LGA-543001
Akwa Ibom State Nigeria-W/A
Tel. 08036693841
Email: ksslibrary@eteroyalmail.com

READ AT LEAST SEVEN LECTURE'S REVELATIONS BEFORE YOU CAN MAKE ANY COMMENTS
In the Name of Our Lord Jesus Christ In the Blood of Our Lord Jesus Christ
Now and forever more

Everybody should have access and read at least seven **FATHER'S TALK (GOD PRESENT)** Lecture's Revelations before you can make any comments about it. If you do not go through at least seven **FATHER'S TALK** lectures and you comment you may make mistakes. When you make mistakes your blood will be upon you because you would have taken voluntary evolution to misquote **THE FATHER GOD THE CREATOR OF THE UNIVERSE.** If however, you go through any seven of **THE FATHER'S TALK (GOD PRESENT)** –

Information

one of **THE FATHER'S TALK** stands for one Spirit of God, which means that **FATHER'S TALK GOD PRESENT** Lectures Revelation are witness by the Seven Spirits of God, which **I** use as the Seven Church of God and Seven days of the Week, Seven spirits of Creations in one Supreme energy of THE FATHER GOD, THE SPOKEN WORD. When you read seven **FATHER'S TALK** Lectures then, **I THE FATHER GOD** will reveal you as positive person. Then you will have a portion in **ME**. One of **THE FATHER'S TALK** will have a portion in you. Then you would know that this information came from **THE FATHER GOD.**
The Father's Talk God Present is not a mere talk from a mere man!
In the Name of Our Lord Jesus Christ In the Blood of Our Lord Jesus Christ, Now and forever more

WWW.THEWORDCITY.COM
THE UNIVERSAL

SUPREME ACKNOWLEDGEMENT

'THE ONLY SOURCE AND REMEDY TO END ALL HUMANITIES PROBLEMS'

Join me to Celebrate; Acknowledge, Appreciates and give full RECOGNITION to THE UNIVERSAL SUPREME WORD, YOUR LIFE FORCE, THE TOTALITY OF ALL TOTALITIES YOUR CREATOR, THE FATHER GOD ALMIGHTY,

Information

Information

THE CREATOR OF THE UNIVERSE

WWW.COME4WORD.COM
Contact EMAIL:
hrmkingsolomon@eteroyalmail.com

THANK YOU FATHER

ESTABLISH MY SPIRITUAL LIBRARY

I THE FATHER GOD ALMIGHTY THE SUPREME WORD OF THE UNIVERSE AM THE SPIRITUAL FOOD TO FEED YOUR SOUL. Therefore, **I** want every family in this world, every home in this world, every office, government offices, monarchies, countries, states, regions, counties, communities, local authorities compound, family homes, everyone everywhere should be collecting published copies of **THE EVERLASTING GOSPEL AND THE FATHER'S TALK (GOD PRESENT)** Lectures Revelations of KING SOLOMON SPIRITUAL LIBRARY should be established physically in your houses. So that everybody should have those RECORDS. Go to read the books regularly. Every family should have this Library **MY INFORMATION CENTRE** for their family members.

Every generation of the particular family could easily go to their family Library of KING SOLOMON SPIRITUAL LIBRARY EVERLASTING GOSPEL and the **FATHER'S TALK (GOD PRESENT) Lectures Revelations** and read the Gospels and Lectures Revelations. Generations upon generations will access their KING SOLOMON SPIRITUAL LIBRARY.

You must all have **THE LIBRARY OF THE FATHER GOD ALMIGHTY** called **KING SOLOMON SPIRITUAL LIBRARY FATHER'S TALK (GOD PRESENT) LECTURES REVELATIONS** in your homes and offices. The authorities and individuals concerned must see to that. When you establish your branch of KING SOLOMON SPIRITUAL LIBRARY and have Everlasting Gospels and the **FATHER'S TALK (GOD PRESENT)** Lectures Revelations that place is blessed and secured. In the name and Blood of Our

Lord Jesus Christ, now and forever more. Amen.

THANK YOU FATHER

Information

The title List of some of the
Father's Talk
(GOD Present)

1: THE MANUAL OF THE SPOKEN WORD

2: THE MANUAL OF LIFE

3: INVESTMENT WITH GOD

4: ISO IBOT EDEM IBOT

5: THE CHARACTER OF THE NEW WORLD

6: HELPMANTRANS

7: UNDERSTANDING MY WORD

8: TRUTH, POSITION, POST AND NAME

9: NON STOP BLESSING

10: IMPRESSION

11: STAGES OF EDUCATIONS (SPE, SSE & SUE)

12: THE ENGINEERING OF LIFE

13: THE CONTENT PACKAGE

14: THE BUDGET OF THE NEW WORLD

15: DIVINE ATTENTION

16: THE BABY SPIRIT

17: PROMOTION

18: ADVANCE AND PROGRESSING MIND

19: THE TEMPLE OF THE LIVING GOD

20: I AM OK

21: THE SPIRIT OF TRUTH

22: THE PERFECT PERMANENCY

23: THE FATHER GOD, GOD, GOD THE FATHER

24: HUSBAND, WIFE AND CHILD

25: GOD AND HIS HARBINGER

26: LIFE EVERLASTING

27: POSSESS

28: MY MIND AND MY PLAN

29: AFTER HEART AND AFTER MIND

30: MY DECLARATION & STAND IN BCS

31: BEYOND THE HOPE OF FAITH

32: MENTAL STAIN

33: THE PRINCIPLE OF SELF HOLD

34: THE MASTERSHIP

35: HIDU-CUM

36: THE UNIVERSAL PARENT

37: ADVANCED YOU AND ME

38: THE GREAT UNIVERSAL CHANGE

39: THE PROJECTED MIND
40: INDESTRUCTIBLE BLESSED FIVE STARS

41: ASTROTS, GOD PRESENT I AND MY FATHER

42: SONGS THE COMPLETION

43: THE RIGHT BUTTON

44: AKWA ABASI IBOM- ETE - DIRECTING NDITO AKWA IBOM

45: THE DIGITAL AGE

46: GOD IS OFFICIAL CHAMPION

47: A TRUE WITNESS

48: MYSTERY OF PROCREATION AND BIRTH

49: THE UNIVERSAL UMBRELLA

50: THE FORERUNNER

51: A OF A TO Z (FIRST OF ALL)

52: MAN IN THREE CAPACITIES

53: THE TRUE LIFE OF HOLY SPIRIT PERSONIFIED

54: IN-BETWEEN THE FATHER & THE SON

55: DIVINE ARRANGEMENT & AUTHORITY

56: TWENTY FIRST CENTURY IS NOT FOR SATAN

57: THE SUPREME WORD SEASON CELEBRATION

58: THE MAXIMUM DEITY

59: TRANSFORMER TRANSMITTER AND WAVE

60: THE SUPREME FUTURE

61: THE BYLOVE OF WORD

62: THE SIGNATURE OF THE FATHER GOD

63: THE TWO WAYS

64: THE UNDERSTANDING OF LIFE

65: THE GREATER THAN SOLOMON IS HERE

66: THE CONQUEROR

67: THE SPIRITUAL GENERAL INSPECTOR OF LIFE

68: THE NIGERIA IN THE AFRICA Part one

69: THE NIGERIA IN THE AFRICA Part two

70: THE CREATOR AND CREATIONS PART ONE

71: THE CREATOR AND CREATIONS PART TWO

72: THE CREATOR AND CREATIONS PART THREE

73: THE SUPREME TEACHER

74: THE SPIRITUAL COVER

75: THE NIGERIA IN THE AFRICA PART THREE

76: THE SUPREME BELIEVE

77: CAST AND BAN (LECTURE IN LIVERPOOL)

78: LIFE EXTENSION MANUAL

79: THE SPIRITUAL TRAFFIC

80: THE VOICE OF THE CREATOR

81: <u>MY OFFICE</u>

82: LIFE SPIRITUAL FIRE EXTINGUISHER

83: <u>INFORMATION</u>

84: FATHER GOD FINAL ARRANGEMENT

85: THE LOVERS OF CHRIST

86: I LOVE YOU, I LOVE YOU TOO

87: THE UNIVERSAL SUPREME UPDATE

88: THE SUPREME ALTAR

89: THE SOURCE AND DESTINATION

90: A SON LIKE THE FATHER THE KING OF KINGS A ROOTS FROM HEAVEN (NOT THIS TIME AROUND)

91: THE TRUE WITNESS AND THE TRUE SERVANT

92: THE FINAL ARRANGEMENT

93: A TRUE NIGERIAN MAN AND WOMAN

94: EVERYONE MUST PERSONALLY INVOLVE

95: BEWARE

96: ESIEN EMANA AKPAN "THE AFRICAN PROBLEMS"

97: THE SECRET OF THE UNIVERSAL PROBLEMS AND THE REMEDY (MUSLIM AND CHRISTIAN FROM THE SAME PARENT)

98: MMU-UDIM – THE BLESSED MOTHER (ABASI ME UDIM)

99: THINK WELL, SPEAK WELL AND DO WELL

Information

100: THE STAGES OF HOW TO PROCESS THE WORD

101: EVIL STAIN, WHO RUNS AWAY FROM WHO

THANK YOU FATHER

www.ingramcontent.com/pod-product-compliance
Ingram Content Group UK Ltd.
Pitfield, Milton Keynes, MK11 3LW, UK
UKHW041257180426
11947UKWH00008B/531